Joyce Appleby on *Thomas Jefferson*

Louis Auchincloss on *Theodore Roosevelt*

Jean Baker on *James Buchanan*

H. W. Brands on *Woodrow Wilson*

Douglas Brinkley on *Gerald R. Ford*

James MacGregor Burns and Susan Dunn on *George Washington*

Robert Dallek on *James Monroe*

John W. Dean on *Warren G. Harding*

John Patrick Diggins on *John Adams*

E. L. Doctorow on *Abraham Lincoln*

Henry F. Graff on *Grover Cleveland*

Hendrik Hertzberg on *Jimmy Carter*

Roy Jenkins on *Franklin Delano Roosevelt*

Zachary Karabell on *Chester A. Arthur*

William E. Leuchtenburg on *Herbert Hoover*

Timothy Naftali on *George Bush*

Kevin Phillips on *William McKinley*

Robert V. Remini on *John Quincy Adams*

John Seigenthaler on *James K. Polk*

Hans L. Trefousse on *Rutherford B. Hayes*

Tom Wicker on *Dwight D. Eisenhower*

Edward Widmer on *Martin Van Buren*

Sean Wilentz on *Andrew Jackson*

Garry Wills on *James Madison*

Joyce Appleby on *Thomas Jefferson*
Louis Auchincloss on *Theodore Roosevelt*
Jean Baker on *James Buchanan*
H. W. Brands on *Woodrow Wilson*
Douglas Brinkley on *Gerald R. Ford*
James MacGregor Burns and Susan Dunn on *George Washington*
Robert Dallek on *James Monroe*
John W. Dean on *Warren G. Harding*
John Patrick Diggins on *John Adams*
E. L. Doctorow on *Abraham Lincoln*
Henry F. Graff on *Grover Cleveland*
Hendrik Hertzberg on *Jimmy Carter*
Roy Jenkins on *Franklin Delano Roosevelt*
Zachary Karabell on *Chester A. Arthur*
William E. Leuchtenburg on *Herbert Hoover*
Timothy Naftali on *George Bush*
Kevin Phillips on *William McKinley*
Robert V. Remini on *John Quincy Adams*
John Seigenthaler on *James K. Polk*
Hans L. Trefousse on *Rutherford B. Hayes*
Tom Wicker on *Dwight D. Eisenhower*
Edward Widmer on *Martin Van Buren*
Sean Wilentz on *Andrew Jackson*
Garry Wills on *James Madison*

Unmasking Deep Throat
The Rehnquist Choice
Lost Honor
Blind Ambition

Warren G. Harding

John W. Dean

Warren G. Harding

THE AMERICAN PRESIDENTS SERIES

ARTHUR M. SCHLESINGER, JR., GENERAL EDITOR

Times Books

HENRY HOLT AND COMPANY, NEW YORK

Times Books
Henry Holt and Company, LLC
Publishers since 1866
115 West 18th Street
New York, New York 10011

Henry Holt® is a registered trademark of Henry Holt and Company, LLC.

LIBRARY OF CONGRESS CATALOGING-IN-PUBLICATION DATA
Dean, John W. (John Wesley), 1938–
Warren G. Harding / John W. Dean.—1st ed.
p. cm.—(The American presidents series)
Includes bibliographical references (p.   ) and index.
ISBN: 0-8050-6956-9
1. Harding, Warren G. (Warren Gamaliel), 1865–1923. 2. Presidents—United States—Biography. 3. United States—Politics and government—1921–1923.
I. Title. II. American presidents series (Times Books (Firm))
E786.D4 2004
973.91'4'092—dc22
[B]   2003049368

Henry Holt books are available for special promotions and premiums.
For details contact: Director, Special Markets.

First Edition 2004

Printed in the United States of America
1 3 5 7 9 10 8 6 4 2

Contents

Editor's Note   xv

Introduction   1

1. Young Harding   5

2. Editor, Publisher, and Apprentice Politician   13

3. United States Senator   32

4. Winning the Nomination   53

5. The 1920 Campaign   68

6. Cabinet Making   79

7. An Unfinished Presidency   95

8. Death and Disgrace   137

Notes   171

Milestones   187

Selected Bibliography   189

Index   193

Contents

Editor's Note   xv

Introduction   1

1. Young Harding   5

2. Editor, Publisher, and Apprentice Politician   13

3. United States Senator   32

4. Winning the Nomination   53

5. The 1920 Campaign   68

6. Cabinet Making   79

7. An Unfinished Presidency   95

8. Death and Disgrace   137

Notes   171

Milestones   187

Selected Bibliography   189

Index   193

Editor's Note

THE AMERICAN PRESIDENCY

The president is the central player in the American political order. That would seem to contradict the intentions of the Founding Fathers. Remembering the horrid example of the British monarchy, they invented a separation of powers in order, as Justice Brandeis later put it, "to preclude the exercise of arbitrary power." Accordingly, they divided the government into three allegedly equal and coordinate branches—the executive, the legislative, and the judiciary.

But a system based on the tripartite separation of powers has an inherent tendency toward inertia and stalemate. One of the three branches must take the initiative if the system is to move. The executive branch alone is structurally capable of taking that initiative. The Founders must have sensed this when they accepted Alexander Hamilton's proposition in the Seventieth Federalist that "energy in the executive is a leading character in the definition of good government." They thus envisaged a strong president—but within an equally strong system of constitutional accountability. (The term *imperial presidency* arose in the 1970s to describe the situation when the balance between power and accountability is upset in favor of the executive.)

The American system of self-government thus comes to focus in the presidency—"the vital place of action in the system," as Woodrow Wilson put it. Henry Adams, himself the great-grandson and grandson of presidents as well as the most brilliant of American historians, said that the American president "resembles the commander of a ship at sea. He must have a helm to grasp, a course to steer, a port to seek." The men in the White House (thus far only men, alas) in steering their chosen courses have shaped our destiny as a nation.

Biography offers an easy education in American history, rendering the past more human, more vivid, more intimate, more accessible, more connected to ourselves. Biography reminds us that presidents are not supermen. They are human beings too, worrying about decisions, attending to wives and children, juggling balls in the air, and putting on their pants one leg at a time. Indeed, as Emerson contended, "There is properly no history; only biography."

Presidents serve us as inspirations, and they also serve us as warnings. They provide bad examples as well as good. The nation, the Supreme Court has said, has "no right to expect that it will always have wise and humane rulers, sincerely attached to the principles of the Constitution. Wicked men, ambitious of power, with hatred of liberty and contempt of law, may fill the place once occupied by Washington and Lincoln."

The men in the White House express the ideal and the values, the frailties and the flaws, of the voters who send them there. It is altogether natural that we should want to know more about the virtues and the vices of the fellows we have elected to govern us. As we know more about them, we will know more about ourselves. The French political philosopher Joseph de Maistre said, "Every nation has the government it deserves."

At the start of the twenty-first century, forty-two men have made it to the Oval Office. (George W. Bush is counted our forty-third president, because Grover Cleveland, who served nonconsecutive terms, is counted twice.) Of the parade of presidents, a dozen or so lead the polls periodically conducted by historians and political scientists. What makes a great president?

Great presidents possess, or are possessed by, a vision of an ideal America. Their passion, as they grasp the helm, is to set the ship of state on the right course toward the port they seek. Great presidents also have a deep psychic connection with the needs, anxieties, dreams of people. "I do not believe," said Wilson, "that any man can lead who does not act . . . under the impulse of a profound sympathy with those whom he leads—a sympathy which is insight—an insight which is of the heart rather than of the intellect."

"All of our great presidents," said Franklin D. Roosevelt, "were leaders of thought at a time when certain ideas in the life of the nation had to be clarified." So Washington incarnated the idea of federal union, Jefferson and Jackson the idea of democracy, Lincoln union and freedom, Cleveland rugged honesty. Theodore Roosevelt and Wilson, said FDR, were both "moral leaders, each in his own way and his own time, who used the presidency as a pulpit."

To succeed, presidents must not only have a port to seek but they must convince Congress and the electorate that it is a port worth seeking. Politics in a democracy is ultimately an educational process, an adventure in persuasion and consent. Every president stands in Theodore Roosevelt's bully pulpit.

The greatest presidents in the scholars' rankings, Washington, Lincoln, and Franklin Roosevelt, were leaders who confronted and overcame the republic's greatest crises. Crisis widens presidential opportunities for bold and imaginative action. But it does not guarantee presidential greatness. The crisis of secession did not spur Buchanan or the crisis of depression spur Hoover to creative leadership. Their inadequacies in the face of crisis allowed Lincoln and the second Roosevelt to show the difference individuals make to history. Still, even in the absence of first-order crisis, forceful and persuasive presidents—Jefferson, Jackson, Theodore Roosevelt, Ronald Reagan—are able to impose their own priorities on the country.

The diverse drama of the presidency offers a fascinating set of tales. Biographies of American presidents constitute a chronicle of wisdom and folly, nobility and pettiness, courage and cunning, forthrightness and deceit, quarrel and consensus. The turmoil perennially swirling around the White House illuminates the heart of the American democracy.

It is the aim of the American Presidents series to present the grand panorama of our chief executives in volumes compact enough for the busy reader, lucid enough for the student, authoritative enough for the scholar. Each volume offers a distillation of character and career. I hope that these lives will give readers some understanding of the pitfalls and potentialities of the presidency and also of the responsibilities of citizenship. Truman's famous sign—"The buck stops here"—tells only half the story. Citizens cannot escape the ultimate responsibility. It is in the voting booth, not on the presidential desk, that the buck finally stops.

—Arthur M. Schlesinger, Jr.

Warren G. Harding

Introduction

Warren G. Harding is best known as America's worst president. A compelling case can be made, however, that to reach such a judgment one must ignore much of the relevant information about Harding and his presidency. For example, Andrew Sinclair, a Cambridge University historian and the first to publish after Harding's presidential papers were finally made available in 1964, reports that "it cannot be the verdict of any historian who has looked at the evidence of the papers preserved at the Ohio Historical Society."[1] Similarly, Harding biographer Robert K. Murray, at the time chairman of the history department at Pennsylvania State University, concluded his 1969 seminal work based on the Harding papers with the observation that "[Harding's] administration was superior to a sizable portion of those in the nation's history"; yet "myths still command more attention than . . . reality."[2] The conclusion that Harding was our worst president endures because the actual record of his presidency has, in fact, been largely overlooked.

History's treatment of Harding has long intrigued me and not because of Watergate (with which I am so familiar). While Richard Nixon's "Watergate" certainly replaced Harding's "Teapot Dome" as the most serious high-level government scandal of the twentieth century, it was while living in Harding's hometown of Marion, Ohio, that Harding first came to my attention. That's where I heard it said that there was more to his presidency than the scandalous stories still making the rounds when I was a kid. Which isn't to say it wasn't the gossip that first caught my attention and prompted my inquisitiveness about our twenty-ninth president.

Early morning after early morning I used to bicycle down Marion's tree-lined Mount Vernon Avenue on my paper route past the home of the former president. Our house was only a few blocks away from Harding's and for about a year, in 1952 when I was fourteen years old, I delivered out-of-town morning newspapers for a local distributor throughout the neighborhood. Because my mother was friendly with a woman associated with the Harding home, which was open for tourists, I'd once had my own private tour of the house. While I found little of interest (at that time) in its historic rooms of old furniture, faded pictures, and assorted memorabilia, I did find Warren Harding quite intriguing. Not only was he the biggest name in town; it was at this time that my young friends, fellows who had lived in Marion much longer than my family, shared fascinating stories about the former president and his wife. It was old gossip that was still being whispered decades after the fact, picked up by young ears from adults and passed from generation to generation.

From this adolescent tongue-wagging I learned that Warren Harding's wife, Florence Kling De Wolfe Harding, had an illegitimate child before marrying Warren Harding, a boy named Marshall, who was related to my friends Peter and Dave De Wolfe. No one was quite sure what it all meant or exactly who was related to whom, so we didn't talk much about the De Wolfe situation.[3] Far more discussion focused on an old lady (or so she seemed at the time) who was once known to be the most beautiful woman in Marion and had been Harding's mistress. Her name was Carrie Phillips and she lived alone with a fearsome pack of German shepherd dogs, said to be offsprings of pets she'd acquired as mistress of the German kaiser. There was also an infamous book we talked about that had been written by another woman from Marion, Nan Britton, who claimed she'd had a child with President Harding. I passed on an opportunity to read my friend's copy of the book, *The President's Daughter*. It was hidden at his house, although he was sure his mother would never miss it since it hadn't been moved from its hiding place in years.

Instead, I asked our next-door neighbor, Jack Maxwell, if he had the book and I might borrow it. Maxwell, editor of the *Marion Star*, the newspaper Warren Harding had once owned and edited, not only had the book but personally introduced me to Warren Harding as no one had before.

Mr. Maxwell knew a lot about the former president. I've always assumed this was because of his position at the *Star*. He knew people who had personally known Harding and, based on what he had learned, he didn't think that the former president had been treated very fairly by history. The more Jack Maxwell told me the less interested I became in reading Nan Britton's book, particularly when he said he didn't think her story was completely true. This from a man who didn't strike me as a fan of Harding's, rather a person committed to the truth. I do recall he felt the biographies written during Harding's life and immediately after his death had gone overboard in their praise and for that reason weren't good history either. However, much of what had surfaced later and destroyed Harding's reputation had been dishonest. While the conversation doused my interest in *The President's Daughter*, it provoked a lifetime curiosity about Warren Harding.

In the fifty years that have followed that conversation I've read (if not acquired) almost every book written about Harding, from the early hagiographies to putative insider accounts, including *The President's Daughter*, as well as the biographies and histories relating to his presidency. Given the amount of study and scholarship available on other presidents, there is comparatively little on Harding. This shortage, though, is consistent with Harding's place in history. Few presidents have fallen from adulation to excoriation as fast as Harding did after his death in office on August 2, 1923. Harding was president only 882 days.* While in office, Harding had his critics, as do all presidents, but few presidents have experienced the unrequited attacks and reprisals visited on one of the most kindly men to ever occupy the Oval Office. It hasn't been pretty. But I'm getting ahead of the story.

My undertaking has not been to challenge or catalogue all those who have gotten it wrong about Harding, only to get it right. Yet when assembling my narrative, I found myself often addressing, and flagging, the distorted and false Harding history, not because I want to write a brief for Warren Harding, but rather because I was curious to discern as best I could the truth of who he was, how he was elected, and how he operated and performed as president of the United States.

---

* A full four-year term, of course, runs 1,461 days. For comparison six other presidents have served less than a full term: William H. Harrison (31 days), James Garfield (199 days), Zachary Taylor (492 days), Gerald R. Ford (896 days), Millard Fillmore (963 days), and John F. Kennedy (1,034 days).

1

Young Harding

Warren Harding's life began as the Civil War was ending. In the winter of 1864, George Tyron Harding, a Union solider—a fifer who had once shaken President Lincoln's hand at the White House—was sent home to the Harding family farm near Blooming Grove, Ohio, and his new wife, Phoebe Elizabeth Dickerson, to recover from jaundice. The war was over before Tyron could return to his troops, and much to Phoebe's relief, for she was carrying their first son, who arrived on November 2, 1865. Phoebe wanted to name him Winfield but her husband preferred a family name: Warren Gamaliel. Warren was Tyron's grandmother's maiden name, and Gamaliel an uncle's name that would prove to be prophetic. In the Bible, Gamaliel was noted for counseling moderation and calmness.

Warren was the eldest of eight children with two dying during childhood. The Harding family, closely knit and loving, was described by one observer as "a splendid state of harmony." While Winnie was still a baby, Tyron and Phoebe moved to their own small house also located on the Harding family farm property. By age four Harding was reading. Phoebe instructed her son using printed letters and word cards from her Sunday school class. Harding's precociousness was striking: "A born talker, the boy was encouraged to enter his first oratorical contest at age four. A year later, when he heard bells toll, he piped up, 'They're ringing for [George] Washington. Some day they will ring for me.' Phoebe repeatedly predicted that he would become President."[1] The child also had his father's musical ear and talent, which could be heard by all the neighboring farmers when he was given a cornet at age nine.

Tyron and Phoebe Harding wanted more for themselves and their children than life on a farm. Both studied and practiced homeopathic medicine. Tyron started reading medicine in the office of a local doctor while his son was an infant. Medical education at the time was commenced by studying with a local physician for about three years before going to medical school.[2] After completing his medical training Harding's father both farmed and practiced medicine until the family moved to the small rural town of Caledonia, where Dr. Harding developed his medical practice. Phoebe, who commenced her studies a few years after her husband, developed an active rural and town practice as a midwife. Throughout his early years, as the eldest boy, Harding worked on the farm, an experience from which he drew understanding for this difficult business, and later, as president, he recognized their special problems.

Dr. Harding was frequently paid by his patients with livestock, farm tools, or land. As a result he became an active trader and an inveterate (although not highly successful) investor. By 1876 the father of a future president had acquired an ownership interest in a local newspaper, the *Caledonia Argus*. This investment profoundly influenced his son's life. At the *Argus*, as an eleven-year-old boy, young Harding was introduced to the newspaper business when his father apprenticed him as a part-time printer's devil. Given the boy's facility with words, he quickly learned to set type. After assisting the *Argus* editor to prepare a difficult outside printing job, needed overnight by a local lawyer, Warren was rewarded with a printer's ruler—a 13-em makeup ruler—once known in the craft as the tool of a full-fledged printer. It became a prized possession and his good luck charm, which he kept with him the rest of his life.[3]

Formal education for all the Harding children started in Caledonia's one-room schoolhouse, where they studied reading, writing, spelling, mathematics, history, and geography. A standard text of the day was the McGuffey's *Readers*, described appropriately as "firmly didactic little books that formed the moralistic attitudes of generations of Americans."[4] McGuffey's *Readers* (there are seven of them) introduced the Harding children to important writers and thinkers, including Harding's first heroes, Napoleon Bonaparte and Alexander Hamilton, with Hamilton later becoming a frequent and favorite subject of Harding's Chautauqua circuit speeches.

School was not a great challenge for young Harding. His father told an interviewer during his son's 1920 campaign for the White House, "He studied his lessons, I don't know when. I never caught him at it and it used to worry me, so I asked his teacher what Warren was doing to bring in such decent reports when he didn't seem to work. 'Oh, he's just naturally smart,' his teacher said."[5] Jack Warwick, a schoolmate and friend of Harding's, confirms the ease with which he went through his schoolwork.

At fourteen years of age, in the fall of 1879, Warren entered Ohio Central College (no longer in existence), located in Iberia, Ohio. The teenager was a gangling but strong fellow, already six feet tall, with an olive complexion, blue eyes, and wavy black hair. He worked his way through college by painting houses and barns, and, during the summers, doing heavy construction work on railroad gradings. In fact, his sister Charity later claimed that Warren had worked too hard: "During vacation days he helped neighbors thrash their grain and worked with all the men, and did as much as anyone, but he was only fourteen years old. He plowed and looked after much of the orchard work at this time on our farm. He helped with the construction work on the Ohio Central Railroad. . . . He worked hard every day, in fact too hard for one so young. I have often thought, and so did he, after he was older, that such heavy work (when so young and developing so rapidly) was not conducive to a strong physical foundation for after life."[6]

As a college student Harding most enjoyed his courses in literature and philosophy. Frank Harris, his college roommate, remembered he loved reading "the masters of English prose." Other subjects were easily ignored until the last minute for Harding was good at cramming. Harris says his roommate would "sit down with his face to the wall, head in hands and soak [a subject] up. Then when he was through, he would jump up with a yell and shout, 'Now, darn it, I've got you,' and slam the book against the wall."[7] Foreshadowing his business career, Harding and Harris launched a college newspaper their last year at Ohio Central College, calling it the *Iberia Spectator*, addressing it to the entire town of Iberia. Francis Russell, a Harding biographer often critical of his subject, praises the *Iberia Spectator*: "For the two young editors the little four-page journal was a creditable production, as lively as many a county paper, full of local items and jokes and advertisements, its editorials ranging over such varied topics as the anti-polygamy bill [in the U.S. Congress] and the aurora borealis. It was a popular venture. 'The *Spectator*,' Harding noted editorially, 'is taken by every family in our city excepting a few stingy old grumblers who take no more interest in home enterprise than a mule takes in a hive of bees.'"[8]

According to Harris, his handsome roommate knew every pretty girl within five miles of the college, and they "frolicked together as innocently as young pups." Warren's mother, not to mention his sisters, had instructed him well on the ways and wiles of women. Warren enjoyed the company of women and they liked this tall, dark, and handsome man who talked and thought so dearly of his mother. Harding visited his mother every Sunday to bring her a bouquet of flowers. When he was later too far away to visit he arranged to have flowers delivered, a practice that continued throughout her lifetime. Childhood friend and later a Federal

Reserve Board governor David R. Crissinger recalled the influence Harding's mother had on her son. "The affection between them was one of the most beautiful things in Mr. Harding's career. She was an extremely religious soul, and the strong religious and ethical feeling which is so evident in all that President Harding wrote was inherited from her."[9]

During his last year at college Harding's family moved to Marion, Ohio, which was about six miles from Caledonia. Upon his graduation in 1882, at seventeen years of age, he joined his family in Marion. With a population of 4,000, it was a true "city" for the young country lad with its roller-skating rink, pool hall, taverns, and even a couple of brothels. The town, which was served by three railroads, was booming and Dr. Harding's practice quickly flourished; he was soon earning $500 a month (equivalent to about $8,600 per month today), enabling the purchase of "a fine house" in the center of town.[10]

When Warren joined his family in Marion he needed a job, not to mention a career. He had no idea what to do with his life. He later explained, "I did what was very much in practice at the time—turned to teaching, in my abundant fullness of knowledge, having just come out of college."[11] He taught grade-school pupils at a one-room schoolhouse just north of Marion for one term. As he told his aunt in a February 12, 1883, letter, teaching was not going to be his profession: "Next Friday, one week, . . . forever my career as a pedagogue will close, and—oh, the joy! I believe my calling to be in some other sphere and will follow out the belief. I sincerely hope that my Winter's labors are not lost but that those with whom I labored are somewhat benefited. How often it is that one's most arduous toils are without appreciation! I will never teach again without better (a good deal, too) wages, and an advanced school."[12]

After his brief teaching stint Harding tried the law. He spent several months reading *Blackstone's Commentaries,* which was how legal education was pursued at the time. But he found it slow going and he was anxious to earn a living. To make some money he organized a band while selling casualty insurance. Harding's Marion Citizens Band gained both local and statewide notoriety, which provided Harding with some money to invest in his future. He learned that the *Marion Star,* a daily newspaper that had been operating about seven years with only marginal success, was about to be auctioned off at a sheriff's sale. The idea of owning and running the newspaper appealed greatly to the nineteen-year-old looking for work. But even with the help of his friend Jack Warwick, who was interested in joining him, they didn't have the $300 necessary to make the acquisition. Warren could invest $100 but Warwick had nothing. With the addition of another partner, John O. "Jack" Sickle (who loaned Warwick $100), and the willingness of Dr. Harding to cosign the note, they closed the deal. Harding became the editor and publisher, as well as an officer in the newly formed Star Publishing Company.

Of all the acquired assets, the most valuable was an unlimited railroad pass. Harding could travel anywhere on any railroad, and in June 1884, the *Star's* rookie editor headed for Chicago and the Republican National Convention. Although he couldn't vote (for another year and a half), and he knew nothing about nominating conventions, Harding and his partners agreed that the people of Marion had to take their newspaper seriously, and attending the GOP convention was a serious undertaking. It was also an adventure that had to be a transforming if not a defining event in Harding's life.

Chicago buzzed with the latest transportation and communications technology. The GOP convention was held at the state-of-the-art Interstate Industrial Exposition Building. The young, small-town editor had never seen anything as grand. He rubbed shoulders with reporters, writers, and editors from the national wire services and magazines, and elite newsmen from all over the country. The cavernous meeting hall, elaborately festooned with flags and bunting, was packed with excited spectators filling the galleries and determined delegates from all the states filling the convention floor. For his first convention, 1884 was a thriller, no doubt a mesmerizing political experience for Harding with its drama, pageantry, and conflict.

President Chester Arthur was rumored ill but wasn't standing aside.* The favorite of the convention was Secretary of State James G. Blaine, a former senator from Maine. His leading opponent was the young New York State assemblyman Theodore Roosevelt, who was attending his first GOP convention and determined to block Blaine, because he did not like his financial dealings. Roosevelt was an energetic and sympathetic figure who had lost both his mother and his wife only a few months earlier and, to blunt his personal pain, was burying himself in his passion for politics. In a move to cut off a stampede of the Blaine forces, Henry Cabot Lodge of Massachusetts nominated a black man from Mississippi, John R. Lynch, to be temporary chairman of the convention, with Roosevelt giving an electrifying nominating speech. It worked and temporarily checked the Blaine machine. But not for long.

Robert G. Ingersoll of Illinois, considered by some the foremost orator and political speech maker of his time, delivered the nominating speech that surely captivated young Harding, as it did the assembled delegates. Ingersoll roared: "Like an armed warrior, like a plumed knight, James G. Blaine marched down the halls of the American Congress and threw his shining lance full and fair against the brazen foreheads of the defamers of his country and the maligns of his honor. . . . Gentlemen of the convention, in the name of the great Republic, the only republic that ever existed upon this earth; in the name of all her defenders and of all her

---

* President Arthur was secretly suffering from the same debilitating (nausea, depression, and inertness) and ultimately fatal kidney ailment—Bright's disease—that had taken the life of Theodore Roosevelt's beloved wife Alice only months earlier.

supporters . . . Illinois, Illinois nominates for the next President of
this country, that prince of parliamentarians, that leader of leaders, James G. Blaine."[13] Blaine had the votes and won the nomination. Most delegates were delighted. But many Republicans were
so upset that they bolted from the party. Theodore Roosevelt's
decision not to join these disaffected "mugwumps," as they were
derisively called, appears to have impressed young Harding (later
an unfailing party stalwart), for it garnered Roosevelt considerable
newspaper praise for remaining true to his party.

Harding had been wowed by the "plumed knight," James
Blaine, and hurried back to Marion to "put the whole weight of
the *Star*" behind the GOP presidential candidate.[14] When he
arrived home, however, he discovered he was no longer an editor
and publisher. The *Star* was back in the hands of the sheriff. Security for the note to purchase the *Star* had been claimed in an un-
related judgment. So the short-lived deal was canceled. Harding's
newspaper career appeared ended before it had started.

2

Editor, Publisher, and Apprentice Politician

It took only a few months for Harding to acquire the *Marion Star* with the help of his father in November 1884. It proved the best investment Dr. Harding ever made. Harding friends Jack Warwick and Jack Sickle soon pulled out of the venture, leaving Harding alone to take on the business risk, buy the newsprint and ink, set the type, run the presses, write the articles, and sell advertising. For a while, Warwick assisted on the editorial side. And as soon as Harding made it a viable business he acquired new presses, installed a telegraphic news line, and hired reporters with a nose for local, regional, and state news. By 1890 the *Star* had become a respectable six-page daily with an eight-page Sunday edition. It was Marion's only daily, and it would prosper and grow along with the town.

To pick up government printing jobs Harding also started a weekly newspaper, which was much more partisan than the *Star*. Harding wanted the daily *Star* free of partisan bent. But the *Weekly Star* was solidly Republican, fiercely partisan, and regularly took on rival Democratic publications. As a result, the Star Publishing Company was soon getting its share of public printing business from city, county, and state governments. Although the *Weekly Star* operated in a predominantly Democratic area of Ohio, it made good business sense for its Republican editor to enter politics since he was able to attract Democrats to vote for him, not to mention read his newspaper. Harding became a successful businessman, however, long before he became a successful politician.

Harding built his newspaper by boosting his city, and in less than a decade he became a leading voice of Marion. His financial success spoke for itself. His civic influence was that of an activist who used his editorial page to effectively keep his nose—and a prodding voice—in all the town's public business. For example, when nearby Findlay, Ohio, struck gas, Harding urged Marion's city fathers to start looking for it in Marion. As electric street lighting became a reality in larger cities, the *Star* first campaigned and then cheered when the Marion Electric Light Company illuminated Marion's streets. In 1889 the *Marion Star*'s editor publicly pleaded for culture: for an orchestra and a real opera house for Marion. Later that year he entered the fray over streetcars for Marion, mapping out which neighborhoods should be served and which need not. In 1890, when Marion found itself with sufficient population to be ranked a city, Harding argued for a municipal government that would enable the new city to pave its muddy streets.

Harding informed and provoked his readers on the matters that touched their daily lives. His constant search for, and evaluation of, issues provided Harding a unique self-education in affairs of government, as he explored and wrote of local, state, national, and eventually international affairs. In the three decades that Harding edited the daily and weekly *Star*, he wrote thousands of editorials. Seldom heavy-handed or malevolent, his editorials were often witty, provocative, and thoughtful. But there was one subject— more specifically, one man—whom Harding attacked relentlessly in his early years at the *Star*: the rent-gouging, real estate grabbing, hard-nosed, and heartless money-lending Amos H. Kling, Marion's richest citizen, and, as it turned out, Harding's future father-in-law.

Harding's difficulties with Amos Kling began only a few years after he'd acquired the *Star* and, before they ended several decades later, much bad blood had been spilled. Historian and biographer Carl Sferrazza Anthony, who has done much to assemble the historical record of our first ladies and has written the definitive biography of Harding's wife, Florence, examined the courtship that Harding's friend Jack Warwick described as a "Capulet-and-Montague love affair" of the future president and first lady. From Anthony's biography of Florence Harding, along with the work of others, a tumultuous father/daughter, then father-in-law/son-in-law continuum of conflicts and clashes emerges.[1]

Trouble started with the birth of Florence Mabel Kling, for she wasn't the male child that Amos Kling wanted. Florence was born on August 15, 1860. Amos was a man accustomed to getting what he wanted so he simply treated his daughter like a boy. During her infancy her father was making his fortune selling the Union army building supplies during the Civil War. After the war, Amos Kling further prospered in his hardware, banking, and real estate businesses. Enterprising and ruthless, Kling was described by a leading citizen of Marion, Colonel George Christian, as "not a man to deal unjustly with any one. While exacting in his business dealings, . . . he was honest and upright."[2] Kling's wife, Louisa, was described by Colonel Christian as "a kindly mother creature. . . . Hers was the sweetness that tempered the more austere attitude of the father toward the children."

Little Flossie was taken to the hardware store by her father as soon as she could walk. Raised at his side, she grew up in a man's world and amid business. Carl Anthony discovered that as a child, Florence had the "ferocity, stamina, and competitive assertiveness" of a boy. The fact that Amos Kling raised his daughter in his own image resulted in a war of wills between them almost from the crib. By her teens, Florence wanted nothing more than to escape her domineering father, and to do so she hoped to study music in New York City. Amos opposed it, but he did consent to his seventeen-year-old daughter attending the Cincinnati Conservatory of Music, a boarding school in downtown Cincinnati where she could study piano. Amos wanted his daughter to be able to earn a living on her own, if necessary. And it would become necessary.

Schooling in Cincinnati with a newfound freedom proved liberating and exhilarating to young Florence. When she returned home following her graduation, warfare erupted anew between a father who still saw his daughter as a child and a daughter who believed herself a worldly woman. Amos was unrelenting. He criticized her life, her friends, and her hours. If she did not return home exactly by her curfew, Amos locked her out for the night. At first she used a ladder to sneak into her room. After her father nailed all her bedroom windows closed, she would spend the night with her girlfriend Carrie Wallace.

Those who knew Florence Kling believe that her affair, and pregnancy, with Henry Atherton "Pete" De Wolfe was an act of defiance toward her father. Pete De Wolfe, a sandy-haired, hell-raising neighborhood boy from one of Marion's oldest families, lived across the street and was one year her senior. His only distinction was Marion's youngest drunk. Six months after they eloped to Columbus in 1880 (they never married), their son was born. Birth records appear to list the child's name (without naming the parents) as Eugene De Wolfe, Jr., although the parents called the child Marshall. Of course Amos wanted nothing to do with his grandson, or his daughter, and Pete De Wolfe soon decided he wanted nothing to do with a wife and son either. While Pete supported the mother of his child and his son for a while by working odd jobs in the town of Galion, Ohio, he spent most of his time drinking. This left the daughter and grandson of Marion's wealthiest man living near poverty, a situation that worsened in December 1882 when Pete simply abandoned Florence and Marshall.

Two days before Christmas, with no money, only a few days of food remaining, and no coal for the furnace, the future first lady dealt with her predicament. Carl Anthony describes the situation:

She didn't know anyone well in Galion, but even if she had, she was not the sort to beg. Then, in the snowy dark of Christmas Eve, the twenty-two-year-old mother bundled herself and Marshall against the cold, walked to the Galion train station, and listened for the clanking of the approaching train. She introduced herself to the conductor as Amos Kling's daughter and for the only time in her life she begged. He let her and the child ride for free. It was after midnight when Florence arrived back in Marion, a night she described as "rough and cold," but fear of Amos Kling's inevitable reaction told her that even in the early hours of Christmas she should not head for her father's home. She knew of an empty house owned by a friend's family near the station. She broke into it. Finding a corner, and wrapping Marshall in her woolen dress to keep him warm, she finally slept.[3]

On Christmas, Florence went to visit her friend Carrie Wallace, whose father agreed to provide Florence and her son a spare room to live in. She was penniless, and concerned that she and Marshall would become a burden for the Wallace family, but she was desperate. Although she refused to go to her father for help, her friends did. Amos Kling, unsympathetic to his daughter's and grandson's plight, refused to assist. But Florence's mother, learning of the situation, secretly provided what cash she could along with old clothing. To enable Florence to earn a living, Carrie Wallace agreed to baby-sit Marshall. Florence borrowed a piano and started giving lessons. Pete De Wolfe's father, impressed with the tenacity of the mother of his grandson, agreed to pay the grocery bills.

Eventually, Amos Kling made his daughter a double-edged offer. He would not support Marshall, or his daughter, but he would take the boy and raise him as his own. Marshall, while not legally adopted, would drop the name De Wolfe and use Kling. As Carl Anthony describes it, Florence decided to abandon her son for the same reason Pete De Wolfe had abandoned her: "a fundamental inability to cope financially and emotionally with the premature obligations to another human being." Florence's biographer says that giving up her son resulted in her "lifelong empathy for those struggling against societal expectations." While she would visit Marshall, she relinquished raising the child to her father, and she was on her own. This arrangement resulted in a rapprochement, of sorts, between father and daughter, but only for a short while.

One of Florence's piano pupils was Warren Harding's sister Charity. The Hardings had a piano in their home, so Florence went there to teach, and most believe this is where Florence first spotted the handsome young editor of the *Marion Star* and where Harding met the athletically attractive, and musically accomplished, young working mother. After Charity started her piano lessons, the *Marion Star* soon began reporting the trips of Florence Kling to Cincinnati and Yellowstone National Park with her mother. Carl Anthony believes that the romance most likely developed during their conversations at Florence's rose garden, which she kept at the place where she rented a room and taught piano not far from the Harding family home. Harding loved flowers, particularly roses. Living in a small town, he knew about her situation, and it apparently intrigued him. "Though [some] historians claimed otherwise, Harding was a stimulating conversationalist," Anthony writes, and he introduced her to history, his favorite authors Dickens, Carlyle, Pope, along with Zane Grey western novels and several journals with literary criticism and short fiction to which he subscribed.[4]

By the summer of 1886, Florence was doing more than tending her garden while chatting with Warren. Depending on who tells the story, Florence was courting Warren, or Warren was courting Florence. Whichever, she filed legal papers to dissolve her common-law marriage to De Wolfe and began seeing Warren regularly and openly. When Amos Kling learned that his daughter was dating Warren Harding, he had a conniption. Amos knew a good deal about the young Harding and wanted better for his daughter. His *Star* newspaper was mortgaged up to the hilt, and the business was barely surviving. Harding had also been critical of Kling's business dealings and relationship with the city's government. But what most riled Amos was the rumor, long circulating in town, that Harding was of African-American heritage. Accordingly, Kling set out to make sure no relationship developed. First he threatened to disinherit his daughter if she continued seeing Harding. This threat had no effect, so Amos decided to embarrass his daughter out of seeing Harding by spreading a rumor that Harding was, in fact, a black—or to use his word, a "nigger." Amos first heard this story from a Harding competitor, George Crawford, editor of the Marion *Independent*, who called Harding a "kink-haired youth." In race-conscious Ohio, less than two decades after the Civil War, such a racial charge was considered a high insult to a white person and fighting words. When Harding learned what Kling was doing, he sent word that he would beat the tar out of the little man if he didn't cease. Kling said he was ready to fight, but it never came to blows. Harding had been dealing with the false accusation of African ancestry since childhood. Such rumors would later be whispered during all his Ohio political campaigns, and they would surface nationally during his 1920 run for the White House.[5]

Harding's papers explain his reluctance to talk about this subject. During the 1920 presidential campaign, when the issue of his ancestry surfaced, his campaign aides prepared a detailed genealogy refuting the charge based on information provided by a Chicago relative, John C. Harding. "It was fortunate," Harding wrote John Harding at the time, "that you were able to furnish the data requested, although I do not as yet know what use will be made of it. I have always been averse to dignifying this talk with attention or denial, but if finally deemed necessary we will stamp it as the unmitigated lie it is."[6] Harding biographer Dr. Robert Murray traces the roots of the story to the fact that when the pro-abolition Harding family first migrated to Ohio, "they lived in the same area with some Negroes, and it was rumored that the two groups were more than just neighborly. Later the enemies of Harding's father expanded this tale by claiming that his grandmother was 'black as ink.' In reality, she was blonde."[7] Other historians note that it was common for pro-abolitionist families like the Harding family to be so attacked.

When Florence heard the gossip she said she didn't care. But her father did, and he refused to let it go. Amos Kling next began an open campaign, using the leverage of his financial influence to make the businessmen of Marion take sides. Either they were with him or they were with "the nigger." But this didn't work either. Harding was popular with the Marion business community because his newspaper was helping their businesses. While the men doing business with Kling's bank told him they were with him, in fact most resented his financial leverage over them. Younger members of the business community didn't give a hoot for Kling, and openly sided with the young couple.

If Kling couldn't hurt his daughter, he set out to hurt the Harding family as long as Warren was continuing to court his daughter. Amos proceeded to buy up Dr. Harding's small debts in speculative land deals. When he had gathered them all, he demanded that Dr. Harding pay them off or forfeit the land. This didn't work either, for Dr. Harding decided the mortgaged ventures weren't worth paying off, and let Kling have the properties. In fact, this tactic seriously backfired, for when Warren and Florence learned of it, they publicly announced their plans fulfilling old man Kling's worst nightmare. Harding told his friend Jack Warwick, "I have about decided that I would rather have Amos Kling's enmity than his friendship. As it is, he now lets me alone. If he were friendly, he would want to tell me how to run my business."[8]

On July 8, 1891, Warren and Florence married. Only those ready to incur Kling's wrath dared attend, including Florence's mother Louisa—who secretly slipped in the back door just before the ceremony, and left before her daughter saw her. The wedding was held in the new (almost completed) home on Mount Vernon Avenue that Mr. and Mrs. Warren G. Harding had spent the preceding year planning and building. In Warren Harding, Florence had found a man through whom she could channel her own ambitions; and in Florence Kling, Warren had found a partner whose judgment he trusted, and someone who was committed to building their future together. However, no bond was stronger than their mutual dislike of Florence's father, and their determination to show him that they could succeed in spite of his wishes and efforts to the contrary.

Florence Harding, possessing many of the traits that made her father a difficult person, may have brought to the marriage more than Warren had bargained for. She was orderly, organized, and demanding; he more lackadaisical and prone to compromise. Florence affectionately called Warren "Sonny" after they were married. Warren called her "the Boss," and later "the Duchess," based on a satirical character from a serial story in the New York *Sun*, with the Duchess in these stories keeping an eye on her husband, the family money, and in charge of all that needed to be done efficiently.[9] The names are revealing, and the new pressure of married life, not to mention life with an extremely demanding woman, soon stirred in Warren his love of traveling—alone. With his free railroad pass, he began attending more Ohio Republican meetings and accepting speaking engagements, without his wife. In 1892, he made his second trip to Washington, D.C., without Florence, and on this trip he met Congressman William Jennings Bryan.* From the gallery of the House of Representatives, Harding listened to Bryan speak, keenly attentive to the style of one of the country's

---

* His first trip to Washington is reported to have occurred in 1888, shortly after Benjamin Harrison was elected president. During this first trip the young editor met with Ohio congressman William McKinley, who introduced him to Theodore Roosevelt and Henry Cabot Lodge, according to an account by a Harding authorized biographer, Joe Mitchell Chapple (with whom Harding cooperated for a campaign biography in 1920).

great orators.[10] The next year, Harding traveled alone to the 1893 Chicago World's Columbian Exposition, enjoying among the sites the exotic dancing of Little Egypt. Florence remained in Marion.

In January 1894 Harding checked himself into the famous Battle Creek, Michigan, Sanitarium, probably at the suggestion of his mother, who was an admirer of the Seventh-Day Adventist institution run by Dr. J. H. Kellogg, "where reverent attention was given to stool samples, vegetarian concoctions, electric baths, and laughing as therapy."[11] While healthy and robust in appearance, Harding visited Dr. Kellogg's sanitarium on no fewer than five occasions between 1889 (before his marriage) and 1901 (while in the Ohio Legislature) "to recover from fatigue, overstrain, and nervous illness."[12] Almost nothing is known, however, about Harding's visits to Battle Creek, but later events suggest that they were provoked by his bad heart.

While at Battle Creek in 1894 the *Star*'s business manager quit, and Florence immediately solved the problem by taking charge of the business operations of the newspapers, and becoming her husband's top assistant (but only on the business side, not on editorial matters). While never given a formal title, Florence remained active with the *Star*, taking on various tasks, until her husband was elected to the U.S. Senate and they moved to Washington. Reporters, printers, and other employees at the *Star* liked the boss's wife and appreciated the benefits her talents brought to the business. First she reorganized the books and records of the business—she knew where every penny was being spent. Then she went to work on the circulation department, bringing the delivery system in-house, hiring and training delivery boys, and vastly improving service, which in turn increased subscribers. While Mrs. Harding never ran the business, her watchful eye gave her husband great comfort when he was not there, which was becoming more frequently the case.

Only Warren and Florence Harding know the dynamics of their relationship: the attraction that brought them together, and then held them together. Clearly, there existed a deep and mutual affection as well as shared respect. Florence wanted her husband to make the most of his life, which was good for them both. Warren Harding obviously appreciated his wife's efforts and indulged her demanding ways, and when they became too much, he managed to find a reason to be away from home. Contrary to myth, Florence did not push her husband into elective politics. Rather, he headed toward elective office on his own, making his first bid in 1895, after he'd recuperated with his stay at Battle Creek. Traditionally, Marion Republicans didn't bother to field candidates in county elections because Democrats controlled Marion County. Harding said he'd run himself for county auditor rather than let it go uncontested; he did, and lost. But he made a better showing than anyone had expected.[13]

From the outset, Harding showed himself a gifted politician, developing his craft in the "Darwinian School of Ohio politics."[14] His talents were quickly noted. During William McKinley's run for the presidency in 1896, Harding was asked by Ohio's Republican Speaker's Bureau to travel the state to speak on candidate McKinley's behalf. Harding admired McKinley's "front porch" campaign, and while working for McKinley he began making a name for himself throughout Ohio. In 1899 the elders of the Ohio Republican party gave the nod to the thirty-three-year-old editor and publisher to run for the Ohio Senate from the thirteenth senatorial district, which included Marion County along with several other smaller counties. This was no gift, for the district had voted almost solidly Democratic for the past half century. But Harding proved himself a vote getter, winning with four times the vote of the last Republican to seek the post.[15] When Harding went to Columbus to claim his Senate seat in the Ohio General Assembly, he was an unknown. But his colleagues quickly found a man they could trust, and he became one of the most popular men in the Ohio General Assembly.

Early in his life, Harding developed a modest and self-effacing manner. It seems he appreciated that he was bigger and stronger, and mentally quicker, than most of his contemporaries. Rather than being a show-off, he professed great humility in all that he undertook. Later, those who didn't know or appreciate his nature read his humility as a lack of self-confidence. A review of Harding's correspondence and business records while building the *Marion Star* and developing his political ideas shows that precisely the opposite was the case. Harding emerged from his childhood with great self-assurance. Because of his health problems, with his father no doubt spotting his heart condition by the early 1900s, Harding willed himself to proceed with great calm and quiet confidence in all he undertook. Humility is not a common trait in politicians, which made Harding all the more appealing to political colleagues. He actually enjoyed starting at the bottom and working his way up. Clearly, Harding liked people, enjoyed the company of others and being part of a team. Rather than trying to streak to the front of the political pack, he found by staying within the group that he moved steadily forward, and others pushed him to the front. Instead of boasting of his accomplishments, particularly among friends and colleagues, he always underplayed them. He chose to be a team player, always ready to do his duty, and soon discovered that without reaching for a brass ring, others regularly handed it to him.[16]

One newspaper reporter who observed Harding's early political career in the Ohio Senate observed: "He was soon regarded as a coming man in Ohio politics. He was an excellent 'mixer,' he had the inestimable gift of never forgetting a man's face or his name, and there was always a genuine warmth in his handshake, a real geniality in his smile. He was a regular he-man according to the [standard] of the old days—a great poker player, and not at all averse to putting a foot on a brass rail."[17]

Harding's career as a politician blossomed in the Ohio Senate. Party leaders turned to him regularly to solve legislative problems, or to put a public face on party business. For example, they selected him to eulogize President William McKinley, when he was felled by an assassin in September 1901. And Ohio governor John Nash found Harding a valuable ally in the Ohio Senate. Soon Harding became the floor leader of the Senate, and rather than rotate him out of office, as had been the custom, the Republicans gave him the nomination again—abolishing their one-term rule. Harding was easily reelected. In 1904, Harding was given another prize. He was nominated and then elected Ohio's lieutenant governor. While Harding had not been the first choice of Ohio political boss Mark Hanna, Harding's popularity within the party gave Hanna no choice. As the presiding officer of the Ohio Senate, Lieutenant Governor Harding sought to moderate and resolve legislative disputes. This post also enabled Harding to do a great deal of political speech making throughout Ohio, and to become one of the most popular speakers on the Chautauqua circuit, where speakers and entertainers traveled from town to town during the summer.

In 1905, Harding decided to withdraw from political life and return to his newspaper business.[18] He would not seek reelection as lieutenant governor. He decided to leave political life because of Florence's health. She had been ill since 1904, when she needed emergency medical treatment. Carl Anthony has assembled the medical information:

[In 1904] Florence's kidneys had stopped functioning. The illness, nephritis, resulted from a "floating" kidney, an apparent birth defect, which meant that because it was slightly smaller, the organ was not stationary. Turned just slightly, it blocked the tubular passages that permits the proper dispelling of toxins. These poisonous toxins then seeped into the general system. If enough of it circulated into the blood, it meant death. . . . Ultimately, because of the heart damage Florence had suffered, [her doctor] decided not to remove the kidney, contrary to later belief, but to "wire" it into place. . . . She was confined to her hospital bed for weeks and then restricted to her room there for just over five months. . . . Her hands and ankles swollen, her hair now gray, she developed a fanatical meticulousness about her appearance and an aversion to being photographed.[19]

Harding returned to full-time newspaper business and Marion. Once again he was promoting his hometown, while expanding the business operations of the *Marion Star* and restructuring the Harding Publishing Company to give shares of stock to his employees. Back in Marion, he became involved with close friends, like Jim Phillips and wife, Carrie, who had been struck by tragedy—the loss of their two-year-old son, Jimmy. The couple was distraught. Harding arranged for Jim to visit the Battle Creek Sanitarium. With Florence still bedridden, and Jim out of town, Carrie Phillips found a way out of her depression in the arms of Warren Harding; she seduced her husband's best friend. But it takes two to tango, and this appears to be the fulfillment of a long-suppressed attraction.

Carrie was said at the time to be the most beautiful woman in Marion. She could turn the heads of both men and women. In 1905, when the affair that would last for fifteen years began, Carrie was in her early thirties (fourteen years younger than Florence). No pictures of Carrie from that period have survived, but according to men and women who knew her, she had a statuesque body and a quick, smart, and tough intelligence. Carrie and her husband were a conspicuous mismatch, for she was a foot taller than Jim Phillips, who was not a particularly striking man. When the blue-eyed and blond Carrie reached out for Harding, he hardly resisted. While the relationship may have started in lust, they both were soon deeply in love. Remarkably, this on-and-off-again affair was a fairly well kept secret until after Harding's death. After Harding died, it became widely known in Marion, Ohio. So it is surprising that it took almost fifty years for it to become national news in 1973, when Harding's love letters to Carrie were discovered by Harding biographer Francis Russell. While those letters remain sealed until 2014, much of their content is known; however, little of that content is relevant to anything other than a love affair that ended unhappily for both lovers.

When Harding returned from his years in Columbus in the Ohio Senate, and as lieutenant governor, slowly, and in spite of himself, Amos Kling developed a liking for his son-in-law, although it was at first a begrudged admiration. Kling told fellow Marion businessmen at a dinner, "My daughter married a nigger, but he's a smart nigger."[20] But Harding proved himself the bigger man and, ignoring his father-in-law's vicious streak, he worked to get Amos Kling and his daughter reunited after her illness in 1904. That too happened, removing a stress that had to be good for the health of all. Kling's changed attitude may be attributed to his new life. He became a widower in 1893, when his wife died of peritonitis, and by 1905, when Harding returned to Marion full-time, the seventy-three-year-old Kling had married a woman thirty-eight years his junior. By 1907 Kling named his daughter his primary heir, and he even sent a letter to his son-in-law apologizing for his years of malice: "This is a duty as well as a pleasure on which I ought to have realized long ago." Most remarkably, Kling began signing his letters to Harding as "Daddy."[21] The reconciliation appears to have been completed by Amos insisting that he treat his daughter and son-in-law to a six-week tour of Europe with him and his new wife.

With Florence back on her feet, Harding grew restless. In 1910, against his better judgment, he let Republican Party officials convince him to run for governor against a popular incumbent, Governor Judson Harmon. A Republican Party badly divided between progressives and conservatives managed to agree that Harding was an acceptable candidate. With the party in disarray, however, the campaign did not go well. Former president Theodore Roosevelt came to Ohio to help out, shouting at his audience: "Mr. Harding is sure to do for you the things that Governor Harmon will not do for you."[22] Also President Taft came to Harding's home turf and told voters: "A vote for Harding is a vote for Taft."[23] But all to no avail. Harding lost by 100,000 votes. Later he wrote: "A hundred thousand Republicans gave me a cold shoulder in 1910 and in my heart I grieved for a little while, but I smiled outwardly the best I knew how."[24] But the defeat caused Harding to recoil from politics. In addition to losing his race, that year he lost his beloved mother. Had President Taft not reached out for Harding's help two years later, shortly before the 1912 GOP convention, Harding might never have returned to politics.

President Taft had been President Theodore Roosevelt's hand-picked successor. But TR, after a few years of big-game hunting in Africa, returned home and decided he was not happy with his choice. By 1912 the entirety of the Republican Party had divided into two camps: the Taft faction known as the "stand patters" and the progressive faction, the followers of Roosevelt. Taft wrote Harding, requesting that he place his name in nomination at the convention. "I know you can do it well," the president wrote.[25] Harding would later say, "I was more honored by that request than I was by my own nomination."[26] This was an honor with a price. Harding had once much admired Theodore Roosevelt, but the former president had actually shocked Harding when he broke ranks with the party by refusing to support Taft. No part of Harding's carefully considered political credo was more fundamental than his fealty to his party. As he wrote in a *Star* editorial at the time, "popular government" was "made operative through the party," and the success of the party was made possible only by "cohesion, discipline and leadership."[27]

Harding, whose career in politics had been driven by efforts to find compromise, could find none with Theodore Roosevelt's attacks on President Taft. In late 1911 and early 1912, Harding and the *Star* had railed at the progressive movement within the Republican Party, which Harding believed was based on personalities, not principles. Harding was not opposed to progressive ideas, such as voter initiatives, recall of elected officials, referendums on ballot issues, corporate trust busting, and resource conservation. But he found the progressives' "unreasonable antipathy to Taft" baseless, and TR's talk about fighting against special interests for the common man "claptrap." Harding minced no words about Roosevelt, asserting that his goal was a personal "lust for power." He called Roosevelt a "limelighter," unhappy out of the spotlight, who had been seduced by "malefactors of great wealth" because Taft was enforcing the antitrust laws. To Harding, Roosevelt was a traitor, "an insufferable boss . . . intolerant . . . an unheeding dictator. . . . His prototype in history was Aaron Burr, the same towering ambitions; the same ruthlessness in disregarding the ties of friendship, gratitude and reverence; the same tendency to bully and browbeat . . . the same type of egotism and greed for power."[28]

Harding's strong feelings were typical of the division within the GOP ranks as the party headed into its convention in Chicago. Tensions were only heightened further when Roosevelt took the unprecedented step of traveling to the Chicago convention to personally direct his effort to obtain the nomination. Upon Roosevelt's arrival a newsman asked him how he felt. "As fit as a bull moose," he announced. The phrase caught on, giving a name to his progressive party.

The afternoon before Harding was to give his speech, he noticed Ohio congressman Nicholas Longworth and his wife, Alice Roosevelt Longworth (TR's daughter), in the gallery adjacent to the rostrum. Nick Longworth was a rumored dark horse candidate for governor of Ohio. Harding went over and, after saying hello, told Longworth he would support him for governor. Hearing this, Alice interrupted to say she did not believe Nick would accept anything from Harding, at the Columbus GOP convention or anywhere else, because "one could not accept favors from crooks." Alice later refused her husband's plea that she apologize to Harding. Alice explained, "That was what I had meant to say, so I did not see him. That, I think, was the beginning of my active distaste for Mr. Harding."[29] By supporting Taft and rejecting Roosevelt, Harding was doing on the national level something he had assiduously avoided in Ohio politics—making enemies, and he was just getting started.

By the time Harding arrived at the podium to place Taft's name in nomination, a week of nasty fights over everything made Harding's speech a bit anticlimactic. Anticipating difficulty, he had constructed his twenty-five-hundred-word address (approved without change by President Taft) to pull the party together, and do it quickly. But with the interruptions of shouting, howling, and hissing progressives, it took far longer than planned to deliver the speech. He opened by praising progressive Republicans as good Republicans, then turned to praise President Taft as "that inspiring personification of courage, that matchless exemplar of justice, that glorious apostle of peace and amity." After a standard Republican homage to Lincoln, Harding sought to paint Taft as a progressive. It was pure Harding oration, at its best or worst, depending on one's senses and sensibilities, but sufficiently entertaining that the progressive dissidents heard him out:

> Progression is not proclamation nor palaver. It is not pretense nor play on prejudice. It is not of personal pronouns nor perennial pronouncement. It is not the perturbation of a people passion-wrought, nor a promise proposed. Progression is everlastingly lifting the standards that marked the end of the world's march yesterday and planting them on new and advanced heights today. Tested by such a standard, President Taft is the greatest progressive of the age.

While Harding managed to place Taft's name in nomination, he did not manage to conciliate the party. Roosevelt, when unable to wrest the nomination from Taft, bolted from the Republican ranks and ran for a third term as president on his own progressive—"Bull Moose"—ticket. Democrats nominated Woodrow Wilson, a former professor and president of Princeton, who was governor of New Jersey. The Socialist Party nominated Eugene V. Debs. When the race was over and the votes were counted, only the *Titanic* had sunk faster in 1912 than Harding's candidate: Wilson won with 6,301,254 votes, while Roosevelt collected 4,127,788 to Taft's 3,485,831; Debs had 900,000 supporters. Taft's loss was deeply disappointing to Harding. But he always had his first love to console himself—the *Star,* where he could openly express his concerns with this election's thoughtlessness.

———

3

United States Senator

Only a few days after Taft's defeat Harding wrote Lewis C. Laylin, the president's Ohio patronage handler, and called in one of his many political markers. It was an uncharacteristic move by Harding to aggressively reach for any opportunity. Although he had become disillusioned with elective politics even before Taft's loss, he was still interested in government service. He wanted an appointment to a diplomatic post, and was ready to settle for even a short-term assignment that could last only until Woodrow Wilson took office. Harding had learned of a vacancy created by the resignation of the American ambassador to Japan. Laylin approved of Harding being given such a prize and immediately went to Taft, only to learn that the post had already been promised to the American minister to Belgium (at the time Belgium did not rank an ambassador). Taft said he was appreciative of Harding's loyalty, and sent word he hoped another vacancy might occur before his term expired, but no such opportunity arose.[1]

Harding despaired over Democratic control of Congress and the White House. He worried that Wilson's progressive policies would result in lowering tariffs, and that this would cause a depression. It was "a shame," he wrote in a *Star* editorial, "to give Europe access to our wonderful markets and spoil years of prosperity." Harding's forecast of a depression became a recurring feature of his editorials.

In the spring of 1914, Senator Theodore E. Burton announced he was not seeking reelection. Ohio had approved direct primaries, and with the adoption of the Seventeenth Amendment to the U.S. Constitution in 1913, providing for direct elections of senators, it meant a lot of campaigning. Burton (who had been appointed by the Ohio General Assembly under the old rules) decided that a primary contest followed by a general election race was too much and "distasteful." Burton's announcement prompted Harry M. Daugherty, Harding's onetime campaign manager in his race for governor and an active Ohio politician, to head to Marion to see if Harding was interested in making the run for the U.S. Senate.

Daugherty, a seasoned political operator, met Warren Harding when they both were speakers at a political rally in Richwood, Ohio. The precise date of this first meeting is in dispute, but not Daugherty's reaction. Over the years Daugherty repeated to many spotting a handsome young man washing mud from his boots at the water pump of a school yard where they were speaking. Daugherty, then thirty-eight years of age, formed an immediate impression of the young newspaper editor. In a state where every young politician was a potential president, Daugherty thought that this fine-looking fellow looked like possible presidential timber. It was an image he never forgot. Harding and Daugherty later became friends, when Harding was elected to the Ohio Senate. Florence Harding, initially leery of the Columbus lawyer and lobbyist, in time became one of Daugherty's staunch supporters. After Harding's death, Daugherty embellished his role in Harding's life, claiming he was the genius who had invented Harding. In fact, as Harding's papers make clear, it was Daugherty who was the beneficiary of the relationship with Harding, not the reverse as Daugherty claimed. Harding's files "reveal Daugherty constantly writing to Harding, giving him unsolicited advice, begging favors, and consistently bringing his name to [Harding's] attention. . . . The truth is that Harding 'used' Daugherty, and it is doubtful if Daugherty ever realized this."[2]

When Daugherty first learned Senator Burton was retiring, he was interested for himself, but Republican leaders quickly disabused him of the idea. Daugherty decided instead to help himself by helping Harding. Daugherty found Harding, however, enjoying his well-to-do existence in Marion and uninterested in running for the Senate. Harding wanted no part of the divisiveness that had split Republicans in 1912, for progressive and conservative Republicans still saw eye to eye on little. Also, like retiring Senator Burton, Harding did not like the idea of a direct primary that pitted Republican against Republican. Long before Ronald Reagan preached the Republican's Eleventh Commandment—"Thou Shalt Not Speak Ill of Another Republican"—Harding was practicing it. Recognizing that Harding's soft spot was party loyalty, Daugherty set out to organize a draft, but that did not succeed.

Yet Harding did run. There are several explanations for his decision, first among them being the death of Amos Kling in 1913. Carl Anthony writes: "For Florence, in a purely expedient manner, Kling's death may have been the great linchpin to finally breaking Warren's seeming indifference to making a fight again for political office."[3] Many in Marion believed that part of the family truce that reunited Kling and his daughter was an agreement by Harding to stop seeking higher office. Others believe that Kling merely convinced his politically disillusioned son-in-law that it was better to build his business and wealth than to pursue public office. Regardless of what, in fact, occurred between Amos Kling and Warren Harding, Kling's death resulted in Florence encouraging her husband to run for the Senate. She was healthy (although subject to relapses), they were financially comfortable, and the idea of life in Washington, D.C., appealed to them both.

Daugherty believed he was the catalyst. He claims he talked to Florence Harding and convinced her that Harding should run. Once Daugherty had her support, he says he traveled to Florida where Harding was vacationing to convince him. Daugherty wrote after Harding's death, "I found him sunning himself like a turtle on a log and pushed him off into the water." This is doubt-ful. Daugherty was not Harding's campaign manager for his 1914 Senate race; rather, it was Harding's friend and Marion attorney Hoke Donithen.[4] More likely it was Hoke Donithen who con-vinced Harding to run, when he agreed to manage the campaign. Retiring senator Burton also took credit, telling his biographer that he was the person "who finally persuaded Harding to enter the primary, and that Daugherty backed Harding only after he learned that Burton had done so."[5]

No doubt Harding was looking for harmony, as he did with all his decisions, but he probably needed no encouragement from any-one. His affair with Carrie Phillips had cooled when she moved to Germany after he refused to leave his wife and marry her. At nearly fifty years of age, with his health better than it had been in years, and no ambassadorial or other appointment forthcoming, Harding no doubt felt he had everything to gain and nothing to lose by tak-ing a shot at the Senate seat—and doing it his way.

The style Harding had developed in earlier campaigns proved remarkably effective in his bid for the Senate nomination. The Senate primary was a three-way contest with former U.S. senator Joseph B. Foraker and Findlay, Ohio, businessman Ralph Cole con-testing Harding. Harding's well-practiced orotund campaign rheto-ric totally frustrated his opponents. Rather than divide and conquer, Harding sought to win (or keep) Republican friends and make Democratic enemies. Harding biographer Randolph Downes found it to be classic Harding: "He put on a campaign of such sweetness and light as would have won the plaudits of the angels. It was calculated to offend nobody but Democrats." Indeed, Ralph Cole became so frustrated that he exclaimed, "If he is not going to fight someone, why did he enter the contest. . . . If a man's not against somebody or something he has no business in a fight."[6] Harding knew exactly what he was doing and won the primary with 88,540 votes to Foraker's 76,817 and Cole's 52,237.[7]

Former president Taft endorsed Harding in the general election,

proclaiming him "a man of marked ability, of sanity, of much legislative experience, and . . . a regular Republican of principle."[8]
Rather than lock horns and butt heads with his opponents Ohio
attorney general Timothy S. Hogan, the Democrat, and Arthur L.
Garford, the Progressive, Harding campaigned with speeches in
which the audience could hear what they wanted. Rather than
attack opponents, he went after the policies of President Wilson.
Harding's campaign style in the Senate race foreshadowed the
style he employed when running for president six years later.

A Harding friend described his stump speeches during the
1914 Senate campaign as "a rambling, high-sounding mixture of
platitudes, patriotism, and pure nonsense."[9] Harding used his oratory to good effect: it got him elected, making as few enemies as
possible in the process. Indeed, he racked up an historic win with
a margin of more than 100,000 votes over Hogan, his closest
opponent, and a victory that immediately provoked talk of higher
office for the senator-elect. Attending a victory parade in an open
touring car with the new governor-elect, Frank B. Willis, a man in
the crowd shouted that Harding would be the next president of
the United States. So too did Ohio papers, speaking for "Ohio,
Mother of Presidents."[10] Harding entertained no such thoughts,
however. Rather, he made clear to family, friends, and employees
that he had reached the end of his political rainbow; he looked
forward to enjoying his years in the Senate, and then coming back
to his editor's desk at the *Star*.

In fact, he would keep his hand in the operations of the *Star*
after going to the Senate. Long before Harding stepped on the
national stage, a *New York World* correspondent had occasion to
drop by the *Star* offices in Marion. "What sort of newspaper man
is Harding?" Charles Willis Thompson asked the managing editor
in a peer-to-peer conversation that never would have been
reported had Harding not later become a presidential candidate.
"He is an easy writer, a fine reporter, a good straight printer, the
quickest and fastest make-up man I ever saw, can run a linotype,

and in the business office he is one of the best buyers I ever knew." The editor added that the senator still wrote for the paper because "in his position news comes his way, and whenever he gets it he comes down here and writes it."[11]

Before taking office, Senator-elect Harding had an opportunity to travel and give a few speeches, or, as Harding called it, bloviate.* Harding traveled to Texas to visit his longtime friend Frank Scobey, once the clerk of the Ohio Senate. Florence did not accompany him when her son, Marshall, died from pneumonia in Colorado on New Year's Day 1915. Rather she joined her husband for his trip to California and then to Hawaii, accompanied by her physician, Dr. Charles E. Sawyer, and his wife, with whom Florence always felt reassured when traveling. In Hawaii, Harding met the man appointed by President Wilson to oversee the government's construction of the naval base at Pearl Harbor, Charles R. Forbes. It would prove a fateful meeting, for Forbes would later join the Harding administration, become the head of a new Veterans Bureau, and give the Harding administration its first and most serious scandal.

One of the first decisions Harding made as senator-elect was to hire George B. Christian, Jr., son of his next-door neighbor, to be his personal secretary. George had been one of the young boys Florence recruited and trained to deliver the *Star*. When the Hardings were married, young George had been the doorman for their wedding. Christian, who worked for his father as a secretary at the Norris & Christian Stone and Lime Company, helped out during the Senate campaign. George would serve Harding throughout his

---

* Harding gave this word its currency in the English language, much to the chagrin of many. Harding biographer Francis Russell writes that the word was "current in Ohio, but long since obsolete, meaning to loaf about and talk and enjoy oneself. It became a favorite expression of Harding's, so much so that outsiders later credited him with having coined it." Current lexicographers define it as verbosity or long-winded oration. Although Harding used the word often, he did so tongue-in-cheek and in a self-deprecating manner.

Senate career, and as the president's top aide in the White House. Many in Marion thought George Christian was the son that Warren and Florence wished they'd had, for he was treated as a member of the family. Christian knew Warren Harding better than anyone, and in time many thought of him as Harding's alter ego. While he never made policy, he made life much easier for the senator (and later the president) by shielding Harding from insignificant minutiae. During the 1920 campaign, a reporter who had been dealing with Christian for many years described him in the *Literary Digest* (July 17, 1920) as "neighborly" and very much like Harding: "Like master, like man. The only difference between Harding and Christian is perhaps a quarter or a fifth. The secretary is that much narrower, that much shorter; otherwise, he is the small pea shelled out of the end of the same pod; as devoid of angles or guile as a buckeye, as pleasant as a lozenge, intelligent, alert, receptive, and as poised as the center of population."

Harding entered the United States Senate as it was making its transition into the modern age. Yet in 1915 it was still an exclusive men's club of seasoned politicians who viewed their primary responsibility to temper the occasionally overheated House of Representatives, approve or reject treaties and presidential nominations, and watch after the interests of their respective states. In the years following the Civil War, the Senate thought itself more important than the presidency, but by 1915 its power had waned under the aggressive presidencies of Theodore Roosevelt and Woodrow Wilson. With the Democrats in control, the new junior senator from Ohio found himself with committee assignments of little significance: Commerce, Claims, Coastal Defenses, Investigations of Trespasses on Indian Lands, and Sale of Meat Products. In the Senate of this era, new senators were expected to keep a low profile while learning the rules of the club, and Harding dutifully kept his head down.

Harding's desk on the Senate floor was beside that of Senator

Albert B. Fall of New Mexico, who had been elected to the Senate in 1912. Fall, who looked like the Wild West showman Buffalo Bill Cody with his great drooping handlebar mustache and black cowboy boots, was a self-made man, a highly successful corporate and criminal lawyer who had served as attorney general of New Mexico before statehood, as well as a justice of the New Mexico Supreme Court. Fall had panned and mined for gold, fought Indians and Mexicans, ridden with Theodore Roosevelt's Rough Riders, and acquired significant property holdings at Three Rivers, New Mexico. Four years older than Harding, Fall took an instant liking to the freshman senator from Ohio. Given the distance and difficulty of travel to Washington from New Mexico, Fall's wife and daughters spent most of the time on their ranch. This resulted in Albert Fall becoming a regular visitor at the Hardings' Wyoming Avenue home, where word soon spread that a bored senator could find a first-rate poker game two or three nights a week, not to mention a good meal. Harding's reception in the U.S. Senate was not unlike his earlier reception in the Ohio Senate; he made friends quickly, and the Harding home became a social mecca for his friends, and they were many.

Despite Harding's low standing in the Senate pecking order, after only six months in the Senate he was asked to be the keynote speaker at the Republican presidential convention during the summer of 1916. Republicans wanted to heal the division between the progressive and conservative factions of the party, and Harding held the respect of both elements, in spite of his earlier disapproval and chastisement of the progressives, who had bolted to the Bull Moose Party in 1912. A groundswell developed in early 1916 for Republicans to nominate Supreme Court Associate Justice Charles Evans Hughes. Hughes joined the high court in 1910; he had been appointed by President Taft when he was only forty-eight years of age and governor of New York. His political philosophy was a blend of conservatism (in economic matters and property rights) and liberalism (in civil rights and liberties).

Since leaving Albany to join the Court he had been out of politics, but his thinking was evident in his prolific, and usually elegant, opinions as a justice. In 1916, former president Taft was not a viable candidate, having never recovered from the political wounds inflicted in 1912. This was true as well for former president Theodore Roosevelt, although TR still hoped to return to the White House. Harding was selected as the 1916 keynoter to be an ameliorator, to set the stage and create the mood that would enable the fractured party to get back together. It was time for the Bull Moose and the Elephant to pull the same bandwagon together, side by side, for without unity there was no hope of ousting Woodrow Wilson.

On June 9, 1916, the third day of the convention in Chicago, Harding went to the podium with a speech he had not written until the GOP platform was completed. He began by telling the delegates they must put 1912 behind them, they had to "forget the differences, and find new inspiration and new compensation in a united endeavor to restore the country." Using his usual crowd-pleasing phrases, he attacked Democrats in general and Woodrow Wilson in particular, while pounding a patriotic drum of "Americanism" and party unity: "Gentlemen of the convention, the first and foremost wish in my mind is to say that which will contribute to harmony of effort and add to the assurance of victory next November."

Harding turned quickly to the events unfolding in Europe, the war, which he described as "horrors that have set mankind in upheaval . . . a tidal wave of distress and disaster" that were producing "violent emotions and magnified fears." Republicans agreed with Wilson's policy of American neutrality, but they were concerned that the United States, the "unarmed giant," had not prepared adequately for its own defense. Harding hit the Democrats hardest on his biggest beef, the same one he had hammered at in his *Star* editorials: that the Democrats had removed protective tariffs. The economic downturn he had predicted in editorials had arrived. "I choose the economic policy which sends the American workingmen to the savings banks rather than the soup houses," Harding boomed, and then brought them to their feet cheering by proclaiming, "The failure of revenues under existing Democratic policy, the necessary resort to the imposition of direct and offensive taxation—war taxes on a people at peace—to meet deficiencies which ever attend Democratic control, the depression and disaster which followed Democratic revision, which were relieved rather than caused by the European war—all these argue the Republican restoration."

Harding's well-received speech caused immediate speculation that he might be the dark horse choice of the 1916 convention. This was not surprising because Hughes was rejecting all entreaties from party leaders to indicate whether he would accept the nomination. As a sitting justice, he could not engage in partisan politics. He was telling friends he didn't want to leave the Supreme Court, and in an off-the-record conversation with Henry Stoddard, the editor of the *New York Evening Mail*, he explained his feelings. "I do not pretend to be more than reasonably well adapted for the work I am doing," he said (with remarkable modesty for a man considered one of the best minds to ever sit on the Supreme Court), adding, "but I feel that I can say that I am better adapted for it than the work of the White House. . . . My reluctance to think of the Presidency is not because I regard it as an office below my abilities; but because I think it so great and beyond my abilities."[12]

Harding squelched all such dark-horse talk. But the 1916 nomination and campaign were prologue to Harding becoming the Republican candidate in 1920. Harding wasn't writing this script, rather the selection of Hughes and the campaign he ran in 1916 helped to propel the junior senator from Ohio into contention for the nomination. A bit more bluntly, the mistakes of 1916 helped

Harding, a fact he no doubt realized, for he spent the next four years in the Senate quietly positioning himself to be a presidential contender.

Republicans, essentially, drafted a distinguished statesman to be their standard-bearer in 1916. After sending President Wilson his resignation, Hughes wired the Chicago convention that he would accept the nomination. Hughes's progressive credentials were not sufficient to satisfy the Progressive Party, which held its convention on the heels of the GOP convention, and again nominated Theodore Roosevelt. TR had second thoughts. He did not wish to be the spoiler again and assure Wilson's reelection. So he responded to the Progressive Party convention by wiring his "conditional refusal to run." It was conditioned on learning more about Hughes's positions "toward the vital questions of the day." Roosevelt, who was not a great fan of Hughes, talked to Hughes and others and soon agreed to give his support. Progressives, however, were outraged with TR, and the manner in which Hughes, and his campaign aides, handled the Progressive Party was the first sign of trouble.

As with all presidential campaigns of this era, the campaign began with the nominee's formal acceptance speech. Hughes accepted his nomination at New York City's Carnegie Hall on July 31, 1916. Senator Warren Harding, chairman of the committee to officially notify Hughes, was the opening speaker for an audience anxious to see Hughes in action. Roosevelt, too, was on the dais as a symbol of his return to the Republican Party, but he did not speak. Harding played his role to the hilt in this bit of political theater by showering Hughes with verbal bouquets of praise. And then Hughes took the podium.

The faithful were ready for fighting words that never came. Hughes might as well have been wearing his black robe, as he lectured like a political pedagogue for an hour and a half. Six years of the cloistered scholarly life at the Supreme Court had sharpened his thinking but dulled his political sensibilities and skills. It was a lawyer's speech: brilliant but academic and even at times pedantic. While many were disappointed, no one was totally surprised. After all, in nominating Hughes, Republicans hoped that the scholarly Hughes might match the scholarly Woodrow Wilson. Indeed, the similarities between the candidates were striking. Both had great integrity and were sons of preachers; both were lawyers and former academics who had been university professors (Hughes at Cornell and Wilson at Princeton); both had been progressive governors (Hughes of New York and Wilson of New Jersey). Theodore Roosevelt thought them so similar that he had called Hughes "the whiskered Wilson" when he wasn't referring to Hughes as "the bearded iceberg." Wilson, however, proved himself the shrewder politician. From start to finish, Hughes's presidential campaign was a disaster. The final national tally gave Wilson 9,129,606 votes (with 277 electors) and Hughes 8,538,221 (with 254 electors).[13]

Republican defeat again provoked newspapers and politicians to talk about Warren Harding as a presidential candidate. Harding had acquitted himself well on the national stage, looking presidential while acting like a regular guy, and his skills as a politician were obvious. Harding wasn't a Jeremiah like Roosevelt, nor a Jacob like Hughes; rather he was a Gamaliel, a calm conciliator. The 1916 campaign, which left the Democrats in control of the Congress, caused Harding's friends to start pushing him to seriously think about the presidency. Not unlike Hughes (who had loved his work as a Supreme Court justice), Harding loved being a senator. Because he had little seniority in a system where seniority was everything, not much was expected of him; nor was there much he could do. He no doubt correctly believed he had a safe and sure future in the Senate. After the 1916 defeat of Hughes, and the renewed public discussion of him as president, he had to realize he could reach the White House.

Harding played politics like he did poker. He was always congenial and enjoyed himself, but he took the game much more seriously than most realized—and he seldom lost. The risks he took were calculated and always conservative; he held his cards close to his chest, and he had a good poker face. The presidency was a high-stakes game and Harding played it with zest, all the while appearing casual and disinterested. As Harding positioned himself for a future leadership role in the Senate, he was also positioning himself as a presidential candidate. He let others mention him as future leader of the nation, but it is doubtful he told anyone his true thoughts. Yet anyone who looks closely at his Senate files and papers can see that he spent his last two years in the Senate doing little more than making himself a potential presidential candidate.

His career in the Senate really had two distinct phases, the first being the four years when the Democrats controlled the Senate, from 1915 through 1918, when he dutifully and affectingly served on his assigned committees. During this period Harding actually was more active outside the Senate than within, frequently giving speeches for his colleagues and winning new friends. The second phase began in 1919, when the Republicans gained control of the Senate. While Harding still lacked seniority, his assignment to the Senate's Foreign Relations Committee during the aftermath of World War I gave him stature, important knowledge, and a significant role in the American resolution of the European conflagration.

No one will accuse Harding of distinguishing himself in the Senate. Had he stayed in the Senate, he might have both lived longer and had an illustrious Senate career. Typically it was the second- and third-term senators in the early twentieth century who made their marks as members of the upper chamber. Not unlike his first-term Senate colleagues with similar low rank, Harding introduced little legislation during his freshman term. If his vote was not important—and it seldom was when Democrats controlled—Harding was often absent for roll calls on controversial matters (and with the consent of the GOP leadership). If he did not have to spend his political capital he did not do so.

Harding biographers Eugene Trani and David Wilson find Harding "somewhat lazy, [for] he failed to vote on more than forty-six

percent of the roll calls during his years in the Senate."[14] While it is no longer possible to determine where Harding was when he missed a vote, it is possible to spot-check, and learn that he was usually giving a speech outside Washington. Such politicking was not indolence; rather he was building for the future. Others who have analyzed Harding's record find him anything but lazy. For example, Andrew Sinclair, certainly not a Harding apologist, notes that "Harding chose to show himself as a casual man. There was a hint of laziness in the stoop of his shoulders and the drawl of his voice. Those who wished to prove his sloth took this manner to be the fact. But the truth was that Harding worked hard and played hard."[15]

By early 1917, the United States could no longer avoid the war raging in Europe. Neutrality was not a viable option with German U-boats sinking American merchant ships. In April 1917, President Wilson asked Congress for a declaration of war, and it was granted. By this time it was becoming increasingly clear that while Harding might not yet consider himself a future president, others did. Democratic senators believed that Harding had presidential ambitions, which he denied. But given his tireless travels to speak at Republican events, and his disposition to avoid taking positions that might alienate him with either progressive or conservative factions of the Republican Party, along with his calculating support of wartime measures, women's suffrage, and prohibition, it difficult not to conclude that Harding was keeping himself prime for the presidency in 1920.

Harding's candid correspondence with Frank Scobey is probably as close as one can come to discerning Harding's thinking about pursuing a run for the presidency. And it was conflicted, and cagey even with friends. Still, Harding's first-person explanations are revealing.[16] Tracing his thoughts from early in 1918 through the end of 1919 reveals that the subject was certainly on his mind and on those of his friends. His inclination was to stay in the Senate, but he did not put a stop to the talk about his being the Republican

nominee. He was convinced that Theodore Roosevelt would actively seek the Republican nomination.

On January 6, 1919, Theodore Roosevelt died. While he had been ill, and heartbroken at the loss of a son in World War I, his death was a surprise, an apparent heart attack in his sleep. Roosevelt's departure changed everything about the 1920 Republican presidential nomination. In responding to a push from his friend Scobey, Harding wrote on January 14, 1919, "I expect it is very possible that I would make as good a President as a great many men who are talked of for that position and I would almost be willing to bet that I would be a more 'common sensible' President than the man who now occupies the White House. At the same time I have such a sure understanding of my own inefficiency that I should really be ashamed to presume myself fitted to reach out for a place of such responsibility."

Harding's friends were not the only ones who thought he should be the next president. Ohio newspapers were interested in Harding's presidential prospects. With regularity editorials focused on that potential. For example, the *Ashtabula Star and Beacon* declared, "No president within the memory of the present generation had a better address or was more endowed with the gift of oratory. Senator Harding would be capable of making the best campaign within memory of most voters. He has the magnetic personality which McKinley possessed, and that rare power of convincing his hearers which allowed Bryan to run for president four times." And a July 22, 1919, editorial in *The Commercial Times*, a Cincinnati newspaper, reported that presidential prognosticator E. Mont (Emmett Montgomery) Reily of Kansas City was predicting Harding's nomination and election in 1920. Indeed, Reily would soon pester Harding and his wife in Washington, trying to make his prediction a reality. On July 31, 1919, Harding sent Scobey a note on Reily, telling him, "I have had a regular nut in Washington several days lately who is more foolish

about the Presidential candidacy for me than you are and he thinks it so easy it is like taking a stick of candy from a helpless child. However, I have not been greatly tempted by the allurements he has presented. The only problem I have at this moment is to get him out of town so as not to have the subject drilled in my ears from day to day." It was Mrs. Harding who finally sent Mr. Reily packing.

Still, Harding continued to position himself as a potential candidate. He delivered a steady stream of speeches, many of which were reprinted and sent throughout the country by anonymous friends, with some being printed in newspapers. Scobey wanted Harding, as a member of the Senate's Foreign Relations Committee, to publicly share his thoughts on the leading subject of the time, President Wilson's proposed League of Nations. Harding informed his friend that he planned to address "the League of Nations problem at the proper time and really hope to make it quite worthwhile." That time arrived in the fall of 1919. President Wilson was traveling throughout the country trying to sell the League, and he spoke first in Columbus, Ohio, which made it important that Ohio's senator respond. More important, Harding needed to publicly engage in debate at the presidential level to establish himself as presidential timber. Few people knew that Harding had gone toe-to-toe with Wilson on August 19, 1919, when the president invited the Senate Foreign Relations Committee to the White House for an informal conference about the League. Wilson sought to convince the committee to support the League, and Harding played a major role in what became an historic confrontation.[17] Harding questioned Wilson several times during the session, with Harding getting the better in each exchange. Wilson could not bluff Harding back into his seat like a Princeton freshman.[18]

During Wilson's Columbus, Ohio, speech he sent a message to the Senate, accusing the Senate of holding up approval of his treaty. This message sent Harding to the Senate floor with a rebuttal. He had been gathering material for months, and Henry Cabot

Lodge, chairman of the Senate Foreign Relations Committee and the one who had been leading the efforts against Wilson's treaty, was pleased to have Harding give a major speech immediately before the final vote on a proposed reservation to Article 10— given its importance in the debate. The proposed reservation (or express condition upon which a treaty would be agreed upon) relieved the United States of any obligation to defend any other country at the behest of the League unless Congress first approved (as called for by the Constitution). Lodge and Harding both knew that Wilson, who had become dogmatically stubborn about any changes to his treaty, was not prepared to accept such reservations.

At the conclusion of the Senate's routine morning business on September 11, 1919, Harding was recognized. Only a few senators were in the chamber. Republican senator Charles L. McNary of Oregon requested that Harding yield, which he did. McNary called for a quorum. As senators arrived, people began filling the Senate galleries, for word had spread. Harding seldom spoke on the Senate floor unless he had something to say, and he was going to state his position on the League of Nations. Many already believed that Harding might be the next president, so he drew a crowd. Because of later events, this speech was the most significant (as well as the longest, at ten thousand words) that Harding delivered during his Senate career.* Fifty-nine senators answered the quorum call and many remained in the chamber to hear what Harding had to say.[19]

His speech was certainly not the kind of lawyerly dissection of the peace treaty that a Charles Evans Hughes might have delivered. Rather, it was Harding at his soothing if not spellbinding

* Harding later recorded the last few minutes of this Senate speech on a phonograph recording in the studio of his friend, Thomas A. Edison. This recording can be heard (online) at the American Memories collection of the Library of Congress, along with several other Harding speeches from the 1920 campaign.

best. The thrust of the speech was his announcement that he could not vote for the treaty without Lodge's proposed reservations. Harding said that President Wilson's desire to assist European nations in order to protect their private and secret deals made during the war against Germany, parceling countries and borders, was not the responsibility of the United States.

"The other day the President called upon the opponents of this league to 'put up or shut up,'" Harding reminded the Senate, then asserted: "Nobody is going to 'shut up.' Democracy does not demand such a surrender. . . . A Senator may be as jealous of his constitutional duty as the President is jealous of an international concoction, especially if we cling to the substance as well as the form of representative democracy." Such remarks caused repeated outbreaks of applause and cheering from the galleries, annoying Vice President Marshall, who banged his gavel each time to stop this prohibited approval from the galleries. By the time Harding concluded, he had the rapt attention of his colleagues, and finished to more applause and cheering from the galleries:

I don't believe, Senators, that it is going "to break the heart of the world" [using Wilson's words] to make this covenant right, or at least free from perils which would endanger our own independence. . . . It is a very alluring thing, Mr. President, to do what the world has never done before. No republic has permanently survived. They have flashed, illumined, and advanced the world, and faded or crumbled. I want to be a contributor to the abiding Republic. None of us today can be sure that it shall abide for generations to come, but we may hold it unshaken for our day, and pass it on to the next generation preserved in its integrity. This is the unending call of duty of men of every civilization; it is distinctly the American call to duty to every man who believes we have come the nearest to dependable popular government the world has yet witnessed.[20]

Woodrow Wilson continued his ten-thousand-mile crusade for a League of Nations. Many believed this trip was the opening volley of an unprecedented run for a third term. Wilson's critics claimed his League proposal showed he really wanted to be president of the world. But everything changed on September 26, 1919. Wilson suffered a stroke, canceled his tour, and returned to the White House where he soon lay in a coma, partially paralyzed. For all practical purposes, after Wilson returned to the White House from his trip he ceased being president. His wife and aides hid his incapacitated condition from the world, and they kept the government operational without a fully functioning president.

Wilson's stroke made it all the more likely that the Republicans would retake the White House, regardless of whom they might nominate. This fact, in turn, encouraged all the Republican wanna-be presidents to get serious in their pursuit of the job. Those who made the most noise, and were already busy raising and spending money to obtain the nomination, were General Leonard Wood, a longtime friend (and once commander) of Theodore Roosevelt's who claimed to be his political heir, Illinois governor Frank O. Lowden, an able executive of that state, and Senator Hiram Johnson of California. The fourth name most talked about was Harding's, who had not decided how to play his hand. Ohio Republicans wanted him to run because they believed he could win, which was good for them. Former Ohio governor Frank Willis and political novice Colonel William Procter (the founder of Cincinnati-based Procter & Gamble company) wanted to know what Harding was going to do because both men were interested in Harding's Senate seat.

Frank Willis, who was thinking of giving his support to General Wood, tried to lure Harry Daugherty into Wood's fold and away from Harding. But Harding, using his considerable political skills, pulled the pliant Daugherty right back into his camp. Daugherty's flirting with the potential opposition, however, damaged his credibility with Harding. He needed to prove his loyalty to Harding, and an opportunity to do so—and show his skill as a political fixer—soon surfaced. Under then existing Ohio law, as well as Ohio Republicans' policy, a man could not run for two offices at the same time. Thus, Harding could not run for reelection to the Senate and for president. In October 1919, Daugherty arranged for the Republican State Central and Advisory Committees to issue a two-part resolution, stating that Harding was entitled to "renomination for the office of United States Senator, without opposition," and authorizing the Republicans "to use his name for the Presidency, and . . . in the event he should not be nominated for the presidency [it] should not prejudice his unopposed nomination by the Republicans of Ohio for a second term as United States Senator." Daugherty iced this remarkable bit of handiwork with a new state law that did not require Harding to file for reelection to the Senate until June 12, 1920, which not by coincidence was the date presidential balloting at the GOP convention was likely to be completed.[21] Daugherty had proven himself, and convinced Harding that he could have his cake and eat it too by campaigning for the nomination as the compromise candidate— for Daugherty was convinced, and Harding agreed, that the front-runners would either self-destruct or deadlock.

Accordingly, on December 17, 1919, Harding made a low-key announcement that he was running for president. Contrary to advice from Ohio friends and politicians, Harding selected Daugherty to be his campaign manager for the nomination. On December 30, 1919, Harding wrote Scobey, "The only thing I really worry about is that I am sometimes very much afraid I am going to be nominated and elected. That's an awful thing to contemplate." If Warren Harding was sending mixed signals, so was his wife. Florence told her closest friend, Evalyn Walsh McLean (whose husband owned the *Washington Post* and she the Hope Diamond), that she couldn't see herself in the White House as first lady, and Evalyn felt she meant it.[22] Both Hardings were in relatively good health at the end of 1919, and after extended discussion with Daugherty, they devised a very Hardingesque strategy: offend no one, make friends everywhere, bring together the factions as the peacemaker, and in the process become the first man to go directly from the U.S. Senate to the White House. Both Harding and Daugherty knew it was no sure thing, yet they both knew how to play the game.

4

Winning the Nomination

No historical distortion has persisted longer than the notion that Warren Harding was an accidental president, a fluke selected by a cabal of Senate colleagues in a smoke-filled room when the 1920 Chicago convention deadlocked. In fact, Harding was neither a dark-horse nor a favorite-son candidate who got lucky. Rather, he ran a carefully calculated campaign for the nomination based on his early conviction that the open field opportunity (following Theodore Roosevelt's death) would cause inevitable conflicts and clashes, if not self-destruction and dead-heat races by the most aggressive candidates. Harding decided he would stay out of the fray but in the contest with a careful pacing of his campaign. Planning and pacing were his keys. As he told Frank Scobey on January 11, 1920: "It has been my own judgment not to go at it too vigorously in order to reach the high tide of our publicity movement until late in the campaign. Some enterprises make such a booming start that they fizzle out later on."[1]

At least nine other men seriously aspired to the Republican nomination: General Leonard Wood of the U.S. Army, Governor Frank O. Lowden of Illinois, Senator Hiram Johnson of California, Herbert Hoover of California, Nicholas Murray Butler of New York, Senator Howard Sutherland of West Virginia, Governor Calvin Coolidge of Massachusetts, Governor William C. Sproul of

Pennsylvania, and Senator Miles Poindexter of Washington. Big money was behind the efforts of General Wood, and Frank Lowden, who was married to the Pullman fortune heiress, had his own money. Wisely, it turned out, Harding turned down all the offers to finance his campaign for nomination. He did not need money to run as he planned, which was to stay behind the leaders of the pack, like a distance runner, ready if and when the leaders faltered. This wasn't a total long-shot strategy, rather a shrewdly calibrated undertaking. But Harding knew no one wins a nomination without a bit of luck as well.

In 1920 only sixteen states held presidential preference primaries. While these primary "beauty contest" races created publicity, they were not taken terribly seriously by professional politicians. Harding refused to run in any primary where a favorite son was seeking the nomination, for he did not wish to offend. Two primaries he decided upon were Indiana and Montana, with the only possible road for Harding to the White House going through Ohio. To have any chance at the nomination, and place himself amid the serious contenders, he had to have the support of Ohio's delegation at the convention. Ohio was considered pivotal in presidential politics—a fact that gave Ohio's favorite son something more than its block of electoral votes. Ohio had a remarkable record for producing presidents throughout Harding's lifetime: Ulysses S. Grant, Rutherford B. Hayes, James A. Garfield, Benjamin Harrison, William McKinley, and William H. Taft. Having produced seven presidents (and four vice presidents) by 1920, Ohio was something of a political litmus test, and automatically gave its favorite sons an aura of significance.

Both Harding and Daugherty assumed that Ohio's forty-eight convention delegates were Harding's for the taking, but General Leonard Wood's supporters felt otherwise. They wanted their candidate to challenge Harding's favorite-son status. Publicly, Harding welcomed the contest with Wood. Privately he seethed over Wood's audacity in invading his turf. To Harding, Wood's challenge in Ohio was another example of the loathsome nature of the new primary system, which forced Republican against Republican. As he told a friend, "I have made it an unfailing practice to so conduct my own campaign that I have never put a stone in the way of the election of a [Republican] competitor."[2] But he needed Ohio; otherwise he was not a viable contender.

General Wood's campaign was being managed by Cincinnati soap magnate Colonel William C. Procter, who was pouring his own funds into the effort. Wood's forces tried to make a deal with Harding, an arrangement to make Wood the second choice of the Ohio delegates with Harding giving Wood the Ohio vote on the early ballots at the convention. Harding wasn't interested, for he intended to have the Ohio vote for himself. If a primary fight was necessary, so be it.

Wood arrived in Ohio and stormed the state echoing TR's progressivism, always wearing his army uniform, which he insisted on doing throughout the primaries and convention. Harding remained cordial, and mostly ignored Wood to talk about his new favorite subject—Americanism, which had become something of a Republican mantra in 1920. What was Americanism? When asked, Republican senator Boies Penrose of Pennsylvania said, "Damned if I know, but you will find it a damn good issue to get votes in an election."[3] Harding's Americanism speeches usually contained exhortations like: "[We must] make sure our own house is in perfect order before we attempt the miracle of Old World stabilization. Call it selfishness or nationality if you will, I think it an inspiration to patriotic devotion—to safeguard America first, to stabilize America first, to prosper America first, to think of America first, to exalt America first, to live for and revere America first."[4]

Harding's nonconfrontational campaign style appealed to newspapers. The Bowling Green, Ohio, *Sentinel-Tribune* provided a typical news analysis of Harding's campaign: "In effect, Senator Harding says to other presidential candidates, 'Come in, boys, the water's fine. Let's see who will reach the other shore first, and be as good friends after the race is over.'"[5] In fact, Harding was so confident about the Ohio contest with General Wood that he went over to Indiana to campaign for his next primary. As it turned out, he might better have spent his time in Ohio. On April 27, 1920, he won Ohio but the primary was closer than anyone had expected.[6] Things only got worse in Indiana.

Indiana senator Harry New, one of Harding's closest friends in the Senate, had encouraged Harding to enter the Indiana primary, which was scheduled for May 5, 1920, only a few days after Ohio. Indiana was the first real test for Harding, because it pitted him against all the other prominent candidates. On the night of the primary, the returns rapidly showed that Harding was getting trounced. As Harding's mood shifted from embarrassment to depression, he telephoned Daugherty to tell him they had made a mistake. Harding had not won a single delegate in Indiana.[7] Harding told Daugherty he thought it best that he focus on getting himself reelected to the Senate and stop this presidential nonsense. He was ready to call it quits. But before he could do so, Florence Harding stepped in.

"Warren Harding, what do you think you're doing," she snapped, taking the telephone from her husband. "Give up? Not 'til the convention is over. You can't; think of your friends in Ohio." Then she spoke into the telephone. "Hello, hello, this is Mrs. Harding. Who is this?" It wasn't Daugherty, who was no longer on the line. But Florence wasn't interested in a conversation. "Well, you tell Harry Daugherty for me that we're in this fight until Hell freezes over."[8] The Duchess had decided, and there was to be no further discussion about it.

It has been incorrectly reported that Florence Harding pushed her husband into running for president. To the contrary, she didn't want him to run, but once in the race she insisted he remain. After losing Indiana big, he lost Montana even bigger. To Florence retreat was worse than defeat. Her spark, her determination to stick to it, gave Harding all he needed to stay the course and return to his own original plan, which was not to worry about the primaries.

Licking his wounds, he traveled to Boston, where he delivered a speech that would resonate throughout the 1920 campaign and history. He told his audience, "America's present need is not heroics, but healing; not nostrums, but normalcy; not revolution, but restoration; not agitation, but adjustment; not surgery, but serenity; not the dramatic, but the dispassionate; not experiment, but equipoise; not submergence in internationality but sustainment in triumphant nationality."[9] Harding, more than the other aspirants, was reading the nation's pulse correctly. Notwithstanding his poor showing in the primaries, he remained a formidable candidate publicly because he was Ohio's favorite son, privately because of the many months of hard work that he and his campaign manager had undertaken to prepare for the convention. Remarkably, no one had pieced together the story of Harding's strategy and very few were aware of his efforts.

Since January 1920 Harding and Daugherty had been at work. They had contacted every delegate or potential delegate they could and asked for support for Harding as a second or third choice. They asked for pledges in the event the front-runners Wood, Lowden, and Johnson became deadlocked and were not able to break the deadlock. If that occurred (as both Harding and Daugherty believed it would), they had collected enough pledges to make Harding the nominee. As always with Harding, his cards were close to the chest. Daugherty, working with a small staff out of two dingy hotel rooms in Washington, D.C., had mailed every delegate a biographical pamphlet on Harding, along with a personal letter requesting their vote should the convention deadlock. Harding's secretary George Christian prepared personal letters from the senator to every delegate Harding knew, or if Harding knew someone who knew that delegate, asking for their support in the event of deadlock.

Daugherty must be credited with creating and convincing Harding of the viability of this strategy. Daugherty had perceived the potential situation and was relying on solid precedent. Harding, a highly sophisticated politician, appreciated the genius of Daugherty's plan. In 1876, when nominating Rutherford B. Hayes, and in 1880, when nominating James A. Garfield, the GOP conventions had deadlocked. In both instances the delegates turned to Ohio candidates, recognizing the importance of Ohio in presidential elections. Daugherty had not only conceived the strategy; he relentlessly executed it, effectively making Harding the only truly available man to resolve a nomination deadlock.

On the eve of the GOP convention the *New Republic* (of June 2, 1920) accurately described the situation: "No Republican candidate has been selected at the primaries. The nominee will be selected in Chicago possibly at the convention, perhaps in a hotel room. . . . No man and no issue may have emerged triumphant from the primaries, but notice has been given that the interior schism between progressive and standpat Republicans has been obliterated." When the 984 delegates arrived in Chicago, 529 of them were uninstructed. To win the nomination 493 votes were needed. Until the first roll call was taken, no one could be certain who had how much delegate strength.

Harding's first favorable break occurred as the delegates arrived in Chicago in mid-June. For many months the Senate had been investigating the campaign expenditures during the primary campaign. As the primaries were coming to their end, General Wood—who by then had managed to ruffle the feathers of most regular Republicans—had amassed the most preconvention delegates. With Colonel Procter's fortune supporting Wood, there was little doubt about who was the target of the Senate inquiry. Senator W. S. Kenyon of Iowa was selected to chair the investigating subcommittee.

Kenyon's findings were announced shortly before the convention and they proved highly damaging to Wood, who appeared to be buying the presidential nomination with his fat-cat bankroll. Governor Lowden was also hurt by the findings of Kenyon's sub-

committee. Although Lowden was not spending anywhere near the amounts of Wood, two canceled checks to Missouri delegates who were pledged to Lowden surfaced. It looked like a bribe, particularly when no one could explain the checks. Neither Hiram Johnson nor Harding was touched by the campaign finance scandal. But it was widely (and it appears correctly) believed that Johnson had instigated the investigation, which certainly did not win Johnson any friends in the Wood and Lowden camps. As the convention proceeded, Johnson's role in the Senate inquiry boomeranged, for Wood's and Lowden's delegates were unwilling to support him when their candidates deadlocked.[10] Thus, Harding's prescience about the front-runners turning on one another was confirmed.

Daugherty arrived in Chicago before the convention and assembled a convention staff (mostly volunteers) of a reported two thousand men and women.[11] He wanted this staff to keep track of the delegates from the moment they arrived. Instructing his staff to appear neither pushy nor desperate, Daugherty wanted to extend Harding's goodwill by assisting delegates to find their hotels, not to mention develop rapport with them.[12] "Make no enemies" was Daugherty's credo as he and his lieutenants canvassed the delegates in search of more commitments for Harding as a second, third, or fourth choice. Daugherty personally contacted three-fourths of the delegates.

As Daugherty worked the delegates, convention officials worked on the party's platform. Republican National Committee chairman Will Hays had assembled advisory committees well before the convention to work out the basics, hoping to avoid the divisiveness that had previously plagued the party. As the convention assembled, the only potentially incendiary issue was the League of Nations. Senator Henry Cabot Lodge, who was chairing the convention (on the heels of his success in leading the Senate's fight to defeat the League), enlisted former secretary of state Elihu Root—an accomplished lawyer—to draft the platform provisions on the League. By the time Root finished, the language was sufficiently vague to satisfy all sides.

As far as Harding was concerned, the entire 1920 GOP platform could not have been better if he had written it himself. It was moderately conservative in tone with a few slightly progressive elements—not unlike Harding. It was critical of the Democrats for failure to prepare for war, or peace, and of Wilson's continuing autocratic and extraconstitutional government. It attacked Wilson's foreign policy as lacking principle, damned him for attempting to entangle the United States in Armenian affairs, and panned his "ineffectual policy" regarding Mexico, claiming it had "been largely responsible for the continued loss of American lives in that country." As for the League:

> The Republican party stands for agreement among the nations to preserve the peace of the world. We believe that such an international association must be based upon international justice, and must provide methods which shall maintain the rule of public right by the development of law and the decision of impartial courts, and which shall secure instant and general international conference whenever peace shall be threatened by political action, so that the nations pledged to do and insist upon what is just and fair may exercise their influence and power for the prevention of war.

While it is less than clear exactly what Republicans were for, there was no doubt what they were against: "The covenant signed by the President at Paris failed signally . . . and contains stipulation, not only intolerable for an independent people, but certain to produce the injustice, hostility and controversy among nations which it proposed to prevent."[13]

Harding was not sure whether to attend the convention. In 1920 all the major candidates were attending, and Florence Harding insisted her husband do so as well, for she had a special reason.[14] They were joined in Chicago by the Harding family (his father, sisters, brother, and in-laws), all staying at the LaSalle Hotel. Florence Harding was more conspicuous at the convention than her husband, who was keeping a low profile. Florence, concerned for her husband, confessed to reporters: "Of course, now that he is in the race and wants to win I must want him to, but down in my heart I am sorry. I can see but one word written over the head of my husband if he is elected, and that word is 'tragedy.'" Carl Anthony explains that her concern, and the reason she had insisted Warren go to Chicago, emanated from the prognostications of Washington clairvoyant Madame Marcia, who Florence had earlier learned about from other congressional wives who believed in her prophetic powers. During a visit with Madame Marcia in May 1920, Florence was told her husband would be nominated by the Republican convention, it would be a fight and happen late, on Saturday afternoon, but it would happen. The soothsayer further predicted that he would win the election. The bad news was that he would die in office as president.[15] Florence never told her husband of these predictions because he didn't believe in such nonsense.

By Friday, June 11, the balloting was deadlocked. Harding had shown little strength in the early voting, never receiving more than 65½ votes, while Wood had 314½ and Lowden 289½. Neither Wood, Lowden, nor Johnson could move one another's delegate and none had any interest in being anyone's vice president. None of the party elders were interested in helping end the deadlock, for they were worried that both Wood and Lowden had been tainted by the Kenyon committee report, which could hurt them at the polls in November.

Harding was disappointed at his weak showing in the early roll calls. For Daugherty, it was playing out exactly as he had predicted. In fact, he had earlier offered newsmen a prognostication that would prove equal to that of Madame Marcia. "I don't expect

Senator Harding to be nominated on the first, second or third ballot," Daugherty explained, "but I think we can well afford to take chances that about eleven minutes after 2 o'clock on Friday morning at the convention when fifteen or twenty men, somewhat weary, are sitting around a table, some one of them will say, 'Who will we nominate?' At that decisive time the friends of Senator Harding can suggest him and abide by the result. I don't know but what I might suggest him myself."[16] Daugherty's remark, when made, was not meant to be prescient, rather factious. He had been irritated at the time he made the statement, because his candidate was being belittled as a noncandidate. As the leading contenders battled to a draw, Daugherty's analysis started to look like a plan, rather than what it was: an off-the-cuff, tongue-in-cheek remark.

With the delegates deadlocked, Chairman Lodge adjourned the convention so that the candidates and party leaders could look for a solution. Republican leaders were confident that if they kept the party together they would reclaim the White House. But given the deadlock, the heat in Chicago, and the fact that delegates were growing weary and wanted to go home rather than pay for hotel rooms on Sunday, the pressure to end the impasse on Saturday became an imperative. Different factions gathered in many smoke-filled rooms, for "[o]n every floor of each of the leading Chicago hotels there were conferences and conferences and conferences."[17]

For Harding the most important conference was that of his Ohio delegation. Daugherty learned that the nine Wood delegates were actively trying to solicit others in the Ohio delegation to join them. To stop desertions, Harding called a meeting of the entire delegation. Before this session, he was asked again if he would accept the vice presidency with either Lowden or Wood. Harding said no, as the *New York Times* reported (June 13, 1920), he was in the presidential contest "to the last ditch." At the Ohio caucus Harding laid it on the line to the delegates; he needed their support if he was to have any chance, and he asked for, and received, pledges from those delegates who had been thinking of deserting him (although several would later renege).

Of the many conferences that Friday night, it was the one held in a thirteenth-floor suite of the Blackstone Hotel on Michigan Avenue that has drawn all the historical attention. The suite was registered in the name of Will H. Hays, the chairman of the Republican National Committee, and paid for by Hays's convention guest Colonel George Brinton McClellan Harvey. Harvey was a newspaperman, the former New Jersey editor of the *New York World*, who had once worked for Woodrow Wilson, but had since become foes. It was Harvey's bitter enmity toward Wilson, then manifest in his opposition to Wilson's League of Nations, that brought him to the Chicago GOP convention, where he hoped to assist in getting a strong plank in the Republican platform opposing the League.

Following Friday's deadlock adjournment, Harvey invited several senators to join him at his suite for dinner and discussion. Many Republican officials wandered in and out during the course of the evening, and Harvey's group attracted attention because there was plenty of liquor, good food, plus the convention chairman Henry Cabot Lodge was in attendance. Later historians labeled this gathering the "smoke-filled room" of Harding's history, with discussion running from about 8 P.M. until 2 A.M., and made considerable effort to reconstruct who was there and what happened. Most of the participants were later interviewed.

It is clear this conference was not a planning session, but rather a freewheeling bull session. Most of the discussion focused on breaking the deadlock, and trying to figure out what each of the delegations was going to do the next morning, when the convention reconvened on Saturday. This group had no power to tell any delegation how to vote. Such authority did not exist. Most agree that Lodge had little enthusiasm for anyone other than himself to be president, but at seventy years of age he knew he was too old. Colonel Harvey was pushing for Will Hays, and Harvey wanted to keep both Johnson and Wood from being nominated. A consensus emerged that none of the front-runners—Wood, Lowden, or Johnson—was going to win because none of them would be able to gather any more delegates. Early on, Harding's name was brought up repeatedly by his only real supporter at the meeting, Senator Reed Smoot of Utah, who departed relatively soon. Smoot's strongest argument for Harding was that the Democrats were likely to nominate Ohio governor James M. Cox, and to prevent Ohio going to the Democrats in November they should nominate Harding—who was far more popular in Ohio than Cox.

As Friday turned to the early hours of Saturday morning, no one was sleeping and rumors were rampant. No group did a better job of feeding the rumor mill than those in the Harvey suite free-for-all discussion, whose participants kept dropping hints to other delegates and intentionally sought to spread the rumors they wanted out. When Smoot left the session in the Harvey suite shortly after midnight, he was confronted in the hotel lobby by a reporter from the *New York Telegram* who asked if anything had been decided at the conference. "We decided on Harding," Smoot said without hesitation and added, "He will be nominated this afternoon, after we have balloted long enough to give Lowden a run for his money."[18] This, in fact, had not been agreed upon. But Smoot was not privy to Harvey's plan to use Harding as the stalking horse to draw the convention away from Wood and Lowden before putting Hays into play, a plan that had been discussed, and reported, before the convention opened as a way to stop Wood.[19] Daugherty never visited any of the smoke-filled rooms. He was too busy with tasks unknown to others. Daugherty reached an agreement with Governor Lowden (through his manager) that before Lowden would let Wood have the nomination, he would release his delegates to Harding.

On Saturday morning, June 12, 1920, Harding was still enjoying a leisurely breakfast conversation with his family when the convention reconvened at 10 A.M. He told his brother, no doubt based on Senator Smoot's assessment, that he thought he would be nominated. After the fifth roll call at the convention hall, however, it was clear the fight between Wood, Lowden, and Johnson was anything but over. With the front-runners still deadlocked, Daugherty and his key assistants were feverishly moving about the delegations scrounging any new stray vote they could find. Their effort was aided by the buzz in the convention hall that a Senate cabal wanted Harding, and the party elders were slowly working their will on the convention. While the rumor was untrue, it provided a boost to Harding, and Daugherty picked up a few more delegates.

As the temperature in the hall rose, and the morning session became the afternoon session, the delegates' resolve to stay with their candidates was being tested. Or as one wag put it: "There is nothing like the imminence of Sunday to break a deadlock."[20] Signs that Harding might break the deadlock emerged on the seventh ballot. This caused Chairman Lodge to stall the convention. "It was time to spring Hays on the convention," one historian explains.[21] Not surprisingly, Daugherty was outraged. Racing to the rostrum, shaking his fist, Daugherty shouted, "You cannot defeat this man this way."[22]

During this three-hour break there was a concerted effort to stop the groundswell for Harding. Daugherty and Harding used the recess to try to keep the favorable momentum going, securing additional support. Colonel Harvey, Senator Lodge, and Senator Brandegee went to the Blackstone suite to figure out how best to substitute Will Hays for Harding. But their plan had fundamental flaws: Will Hays wanted nothing to do with it, nor did he want to be president; the delegates wanted to go home, and many could not afford two or three more days' expenses of remaining in Chicago, but most important, Harding was not without his supporters. Party elders like Charles Evans Hughes and William Howard Taft, who were not in Chicago but keeping themselves aware, thought well of Harding. Believing that further delay and divisiveness would hurt the party and its prospects in November, Frank Lowden released his delegates, which changed the dynamics of the convention, freeing up some three hundred delegates, all of whom Harding and Daugherty had been courting.

When the convention reconvened, Harding's newfound strength became apparent on the next ballot, and two ballots later he had won. When Pennsylvania's delegation voted (at 6:05 P.M. on June 12), sixty of its seventy-four delegates voted for Harding. Harding was the victor. Daugherty described the moment: "A cheer rose that shook the earth. The vast spaces of the Coliseum echoed with demoniac screams. Ambitions crumbled! And a new figure in history emerged from the din."[23] Harding learned he'd won when a Michigan delegate burst into the room off the convention floor where he was visiting with Frank Lowden and Nicholas Butler, the president of Columbia University (and once a dark-horse candidate): "Pennsylvania has voted for you, Harding, and you are nominated." Harding got to his feet, his face stricken with emotion. Always humble, he grasped the extended hands of both Butler and Lowden. To them both he said, "If the great honor of the Presidency is to come to me, I shall need all the help that you two friends can give." To Lowden he said, "I am not sure that I would not feel happier, Frank, if I were congratulating you." Others soon stormed into the room, including Daugherty, who was determined to get him back to the hotel. As Harding departed, he said, "I feel like a man who goes in with a pair of eights and comes out with aces full."[24]

Delegates proceeded to make Harding's nomination unanimous and turned to selection of a vice president. Harding's preference was Senator Irvine Lenroot of Wisconsin. But Lenroot added little to the ticket for he was from Harding's region, and while he had once been a Progressive, he had become a moderate conservative like Harding. Before Lenroot could inform Chairman Lodge that he did not want to be nominated, his name had been offered. Word came from Harding to "nominate whomever you please, and it will be all right with me."[25] When Calvin Coolidge's name was presented to the delegates, there was a spontaneous approval. Coolidge was selected on the first ballot with 674½ votes. In addition to being the governor of Massachusetts, his only credential for the vice presidency was the event that had made him nationally famous: he quelled a police strike in Boston in 1919. "There is no right to strike against the public safety by anybody, anywhere, any time," Coolidge had declared, making him a symbol for law and order.

Not surprisingly the Harding-Coolidge ticket was endorsed and embraced by mainstream Republican publications, while those of other persuasions despaired. The then–Democratic leaning *New York Times* in an unusual front-page editorial attacked the alleged "Senatorial cabal," mincing no words with adjectives like "cowardice," "imbecility," "pigmies," and "white livered and incompetent politicians." As for Harding, the *Times* found him "a very respectable Ohio politician of the second class." The *New York World* was even more openly bitter, labeling Harding the least qualified candidate for president since James Buchanan, a "weak and colorless and mediocre" man who "never had an original idea." The New York *Post* felt Harding's nomination nothing less than "an affront to the intelligence and conscience of the American people . . . a feeble candidate." The *Nation* and *New Republic* were horrified, with the *Nation* claiming Harding was an "amiable, faithful, obedient errand boy for the Old Guard politicians and the business interests they serve. . . . In truth he is a dummy, an animated automaton, a marionette that moves when the strings are pulled." The *New Republic* called Harding "a party hack, without independence of judgment, without strength of character, without administrative experience, without knowledge of international politics, without any of those moral or intellectual qualities which would qualify him even under ordinary conditions for statesmanlike leadership."[26]

5

The 1920 Campaign

On June 28, 1920, the Democratic convention convened in San Francisco. Complicating the Democratic Party's affairs was the illness of President Wilson, who had never fully recovered from his debilitating stroke in September 1919. Wilson, who was barely ambulatory and whose mind was reportedly often less than clear, wanted to be nominated for an unprecedented third term, but no one had the heart to tell Wilson that he was an invalid, physically and mentally unfit for the demanding work of the presidency, let alone a campaign for reelection.[1] Wilson's son-in-law, William Gibbs McAdoo, a successful businessman who had built the Holland Tunnel in New York and served as Wilson's wartime secretary of the Treasury, was considered a formidable potential candidate, but McAdoo could not run as long as his father-in-law wanted the nomination.

As this family drama played out behind the scenes, Wilson was following the proceedings through his new secretary of state (later his law partner) Bainbridge Colby. Their plan was for Colby to nominate Wilson when the convention deadlocked. Democratic Party elders talked Colby out of the plan, claiming it would kill Wilson to nominate him for another term. The nomination went to Ohio governor James M. Cox.[2] Cox selected the assistant secretary of the navy, Franklin D. Roosevelt from New York, as his running mate, a highly popular choice with the delegates. While Cox was not known nationally, he had been a good governor and, like Harding, a successful newspaper publisher.

Wasting no time after the GOP convention, Harding returned to Marion and immediately started planning his campaign. Affable and efficient Will Hays, who had been reelected as chairman of the Republican National Committee, was selected by Harding to be chairman of his campaign. Harry Daugherty became a key behind-the-scenes adviser. The man in charge of the campaign, however, was Warren Harding, who decided that he, like his much-admired predecessor William McKinley, would run a front-porch campaign from his home in Marion. His large front porch, with a semicircular extension at one end, was perfectly set up for this purpose. Harding perhaps had this very thought in mind when a few years earlier he had redesigned and rebuilt the porch. The Executive Committee of the Republican National Committee immediately approved the idea and arranged to have the flagpole from McKinley's front yard in Canton, Ohio, moved to Harding's front yard in Marion.[3]

Right after the convention, Hays and Harding laid out the national campaign, deciding who would run the offices and operations of the nationwide organization. One name for whom Hays expressed great enthusiasm was Albert D. Lasker, the head of the Lord and Thomas Company of Chicago, an advertising and public relations firm, who had been providing him advertising advice. Harding liked the idea of hiring Lasker for the campaign.

Albert Lasker's biographer, John A. Morello, correctly asserts that Lasker's work in the 1920 campaign has not received the recognition it is due. Indeed, Lasker introduced many of the advertising and public relations techniques that have become the norm in political campaigns. Lasker started as a newspaperman in Galveston, Texas, and later left his work at the *Galveston Daily News* to assist William Jennings Bryan, who hired him to be his press secretary after receiving the Democratic presidential nomination in 1896. After Lasker turned to advertising, he progressed from a copywriter to head of the firm at Lord and Thomas. Taking his general directions from both Harding and Hays, Lasker used radio, newspapers, magazines, movie clips, sound recordings, and billboards to sell Harding to American voters. It was a massive and precedent-setting reliance on advertising and public relations, right down to visitors in Marion having photo opportunities with Senator and Mrs. Harding on the front porch, which were then sent to thousands of hometown newspapers across America.[4]

Harding's campaign began on July 22, 1920, before ninety thousand people from across the country who had come to Marion for the occasion. Senator Henry Cabot Lodge traveled to Marion to present the party's official notification of Harding's nomination. Harding, an experienced editor, had distilled the GOP platform material into Hardingesque axioms and platitudes, phrases (today's "sound bites") that were meant to be tasty, if not particularly nourishing:

- "We inflated in haste, we must deflate with deliberation."
- "Here is a temple of liberty no storms may shake, here are altars of freedom no passions shall destroy."
- "The four million defenders of land and sea were worthy of the best traditions of a people never warlike in peace and never pacific in war."
- "Have confidence in the Republic! America will go on!"

He closed the speech in such a solemn and diffident manner, it struck many as if Harding was offering a prayer to consecrate his task. To those who knew Harding, they appreciated the fact that he was merely professing the modesty that had guided his life:

> Mr. Chairman, members of the committee, my countrymen all. I would not be my natural self if I did not utter my consciousness of my limited ability to meet your full expec-

tations, or to realize the aspirations within my own breast, but I will gladly give all that is in me, all of my heart, soul and mind and abiding love of country, to service in our common cause. I can only pray to the omnipotent God that I may be worthy in service as I know myself to be faithful in thought and purpose. One can not give more. Mindful of the vast responsibilities, I must be frankly humble, but I have that confidence in the consideration and support of all true Americans which makes me wholly unafraid. With an unalterable faith and in a hopeful spirit, with a hymn of service in my heart, I pledge fidelity to our country and to God, and accept the nomination of the Republican Party for the Presidency of the United States.[5]

Calvin Coolidge attended the acceptance speech and was kept generally informed about the campaign, but his role was minimal. Initially he restricted his campaigning to Massachusetts and the Northeast. Later he was dispatched to the South, but was not happy about it, for neither he nor anyone else thought that the Harding-Coolidge ticket could win below the Mason-Dixon Line. Thus, Coolidge was not a significant factor in the 1920 campaign.

Harding's opponent, on the other hand, made extensive use of his running mate. On August 7, 1920, the Democrats launched their campaign with official acceptance ceremonies in Dayton, Ohio. Both James Cox and Franklin Roosevelt headed the parade that started downtown and marched to the fairgrounds where each gave speeches. During the campaign that followed, both men aggressively campaigned throughout the country, with Cox even letting young Roosevelt speak for him at press conferences. Cox and Roosevelt had commenced their campaign with a trip to the White House for a meeting with President Wilson, where they committed to make the 1920 campaign a referendum on the League of Nations. They had selected an issue, however, with which the public had only minimal interest. The war was over and the economy was in trouble, facts that Harding recognized and addressed regularly.

Harding spent most of the summer in Marion writing speeches and delivering them to one group after the next that gathered before his front porch. Daily he met visitors to Marion: traveling salesmen, women's groups, the Chicago Cubs, governors, congressmen, senators, and even a Hollywood contingent led by Al Jolson, who serenaded Harding with a song he'd written for the occasion. The campaign's public relations operations fed stories and pictures from these events to newspapers throughout the country. Meanwhile, Cox and Roosevelt traveled the nation—trying to pull Harding off his front porch with their indefatigable campaigning.[6]

Before long, Harding began to worry that his front porch was losing its effectiveness. In August 1920, notwithstanding the optimistic reports, Harding told a friend he was taking nothing for granted.[7] Accordingly, he began giving more speeches outside Marion. Before Harding decided to leave his porch, however, an estimated 600,000 people had visited him in Marion (between July 22, 1920, and the end of September).[8] Records of the 1920 campaign revealed that during "the course of the campaign, [Harding] made twenty speeches in Indiana, twenty in Iowa, sixteen in West Virginia, eleven in Missouri, eight in Kentucky, seven in Illinois, six in Oklahoma, five in New York, five in Tennessee, four in Minnesota, three in Kansas, three in Pennsylvania, two in Nebraska, one in Wisconsin and one in Maryland."[9] Those who claim that Harding was kept on his front porch by his handlers to avoid shooting himself in the foot have obviously overlooked these 112 speeches delivered throughout the country.

Harding proved himself as good as any predecessor or successor as a campaigner and actually better than most: newsmen found him good copy, and editors found that his photogenic image wore well in their newspapers. His use of archaic turn-of-the-century rhetoric blending with his frequent "whither wilt thou wander, wayfarer"–type alliterations drove his opponents and critics up the wall. For example, William McAdoo, who many believed could have beaten Harding in 1920, described a typical Harding campaign speech as "an army of pompous phrases moving over the landscape in search of an idea. Sometimes these meandering words actually capture a straggling thought and bear it triumphantly, a prisoner in their midst, until it died of servitude and over work."[10] H. L. Mencken cringed at Harding's speechifying: "It reminds me of a string of wet sponges; it reminds me of tattered washing on the line; it reminds me of stale bean soup, of college yells, of dogs barking idiotically through endless nights. It is so bad that a sort of grandeur creeps into it. It drags itself out of a dark abysm . . . of pish, and crawls insanely up the topmost pinnacle of posh. It is rumble and bumble. It is flap and doodle. It is balder and dash."[11] Harding's audiences, however, enjoyed his speeches, and appreciated that he was having fun with his words, although he was not as clever a wordsmith as the Sage of Baltimore.

Harding's 1920 campaign was effective and efficient, even by today's standard. Will Hays was based in a New York City office, and other regional offices were located in San Francisco and Chicago, each run by a carefully selected and able operative. The main headquarters' office, next door to Harding's home, became the nerve center and nucleus of the campaign's complex nationwide communications network, housing among others Harding's principal speechwriting assistant, Judson C. Welliver.

Welliver, a former newspaperman, typed out working drafts of speeches, wrote press releases, and prepackaged news stories that were regularly sent to newspapers throughout the country. Welliver was particularly effective at making certain that newsmen and magazine writers received everything they needed.[12]

Before his nomination, Harding was not a national figure. Yet he received consistently good press throughout the campaign, which can partially be explained by the fact that newspapers were predominately owned by Republicans. But there was something more, a special chemistry between Harding and the reporters covering him. It was obvious right after he'd been nominated. Daugherty was rushing the senator and Mrs. Harding out of their hotel to catch a train back to Marion when a throng of reporters, more than one hundred, jammed the corridor; each wanted to congratulate Harding personally. "Sorry boys, but the Senator has to rush," Daugherty told the crowd. But Harding was going nowhere. "Wait a minute," he said. "There'll be lots of trains, but not lots of other gatherings like this." And Harding proceeded to greet each and every man, one by one, many by their first names. He missed his train.[13]

Harding gave newsmen special attention when they came to Marion for his front-porch campaign. To accommodate them, he had a special bungalow built near the rear of his property on Mount Vernon Avenue. Reportedly, once or twice a day Harding visited the press quarters to "greet them personally by name, borrow a plug of tobacco or a stogie, and . . . answer all [their] questions in a friendly way, without evasion. . . . He was ready to pitch horseshoes or exchange stories off the cuff with almost all reporters; and by relying on their discretion and that of their editors, he kept an intimacy with them that made them friendly to him."[14] Everyone appreciated Harding's political civility and personal graciousness. During the early campaign planning sessions old hands wanted their candidate to aggressively attack the ailing Wilson. Harding refused, telling them, "I guess you have nominated the wrong candidate, if this is the plan, for I will never go to the White House over the broken body of Woodrow Wilson." This didn't mean that Harding was not going to attack Wilson's policies, only that he would never make his health an issue. Harding had no love for Wilson and thought he had ruined the country. Harding attacked what he called "Wilsonism." But no ad hominem assaults or mudslinging for Harding. Even after learning his opponent Jim Cox was slinging dirt, Harding rejected the request of his advisers to go after Cox's status as a divorced and remarried man.

Nothing could have tested Harding's patience and civility more than the smear campaign launched by a racist academic on the faculty of the College of Wooster in Wooster, Ohio—Professor William E. Chancellor. Democrats fanned these flames as best they could without associating themselves too closely with Professor Chancellor, whose credentials on the surface looked legitimate. He had written more than thirty books on a variety of subjects. Professor Chancellor was determined to make Harding's purported African heritage an issue in the 1920 campaign, because he believed it made Harding unfit to be president.

He had "researched" Harding, and prepared a one-page mimeographed sheet entitled "Genealogy of Warren G. Harding of Marion, Ohio." It asserted that Harding's great-grandfather and great-grandmother were blacks, that his grandfather was a black who married a white, and his father was a mulatto who married a white. To support his conclusions, Chancellor had gathered notarized affidavits, which included one from a Marion resident attesting to Amos Kling's openly opposing his son-in-law's 1900 bid for the Ohio Senate because he was "colored," and disclosing that Kling had repeatedly declared on the streets of Marion that his daughter was marrying a Negro.[15] Chancellor's broadside had first surfaced at the Chicago convention but was ignored. As the campaign progressed, copies of Chancellor's "research" began appearing as handbills distributed by Democrats, even though Cox and Wilson had forbade its use.[16] Cox, however, was reported to have joined the whisper campaign. On August 20, 1920, West Virginia senator Howard Sutherland expressed concern that the rumor was spreading around his state. Senator Sutherland wrote Will Hays to report that Cox had told a West Virginia game warden "that either the grandmother or great-grandmother of Senator Harding was a Negress."[17]

Newspapers refused to publish Chancellor's claims. Correspondents covering Harding were filing Chancellor-related stories of five hundred to a thousand words, accompanied by fifteen hundred to six thousand words of private information for their editors—who were printing nothing. Harding's campaign and Cox's campaign both refused to give official comment. However, without mentioning the nature of the charge for those who had not heard it, several papers obliquely addressed the story, with headlines like TREACHEROUS ELEVENTH HOUR SLANDERS ON HARDING WILL SURELY BE REBUKED TUESDAY, accompanied by a nonspecific story of an unnamed defamation.[18] There is no evidence that Chancellor's efforts had any negative effect on Harding or his campaign.

For Harding, the most delicate issue was his handling of the League of Nations. With the Democrats running a referendum on the country's approval of the League, and Cox constantly trying to draw Harding out on an issue the Democrats knew still divided Republicans, Harding did what he did well—straddled. Or as Herbert Hoover later put it, Harding skillfully "carried water on both shoulders."[19]

In September 1920, Maine, which went to the polls earlier than the rest of the nation, voted overwhelmingly for Harding. Those handicapping the race were not surprised. For example, the *New York Times* reported the odds favoring Harding had moved from two-to-one in July 1920 to four-to-one just before Maine had voted. By the middle of October they went to an unprecedented high of seven-to-one, and by election day they were at ten-to-one.[20] The oddsmakers had it right.

November 2, 1920, dawned in Marion as a cool fall day. Senator Harding and his wife were driven to the polls, where Florence became the first wife to vote for her husband as president.* That

---

* Daugherty wrote in his memoir that he and Harding played golf at the Scioto Country Club on Election Day morning in Columbus and it started raining heavily as they drove back to Marion that afternoon. According to Daugherty, Harding's "chauffeur was driving faster than usual and barely missed a telegraph pole. . . . It was a narrow escape. Had the collision happened, the course of our national history would have been materially changed." There is, however, no confirmation of this account and it conflicts with other corroborated accounts.

afternoon Harding's fifty-fifth birthday was celebrated with campaign workers and reporters. Toward sundown, people began gathering outside the Hardings' house. It was not until midnight that the final results were clear. They were astonishing. Harding had the largest landslide victory in Republican history. He had won thirty-seven states to Cox's eleven. Harding even managed to crack the solid South by winning Tennessee. His coattails had proved long and strong, for he pulled with him an increase in the Republicans' majority in both the House of Representatives and the Senate. Most striking was the size of the popular vote: 16,152,200 for Harding and Coolidge; 9,147,353 for Cox and Roosevelt; and 919,799 for Socialist Eugene Debs.[21] Debs was still in prison, where the Wilson administration had sentenced him for speaking against the war.[22]

Pundits and politicians offered their usual self-serving read of the election returns. Senators Borah and Johnson saw the election as a repudiation of the League of Nations, yet former president Taft and his secretary of state, Root, believed the returns showed the public's desire for a world association. Newspaper editors lined up on both sides as well. While no one could deny it was an overwhelming vote, many claimed it was not a vote for Harding, but rather a vote against Wilson. There was a near editorial consensus, however, that the vote represented "an overwhelming demand for change."[23] Harding biographer Andrew Sinclair attributes the victory to Harding's ability to give voice to the dream of the rural past by the promise of returning to normal times. Sinclair found Harding's campaign "shrewd unto vacuity" with Harding performing as "a political artist" while "Cox was a mere political artisan."[24]

Lights burned late at the Harding home on Election Night. Friends stopped by to congratulate the president-elect and his wife. None touched Harding more deeply than a group from the *Marion Star*. Luther Miller, a long-bearded printer, the oldest employee at the *Star* who had been with Harding from the beginning, stumbled through a speech they had prepared for the boss.

Before Luther finished, he reached into his pocket and took out a gift, which he awkwardly put in Harding's hand. As Luther finished his speech, Harding's eyes had transfixed on the gift, and tears were rolling down the cheeks of the president-elect. It was a gold printer's rule for his desk, matching the one only Luther Miller and a few others knew he had carried in his pocket since eleven years of age (for good luck). Harding tried to speak but he couldn't. His face twitched and tears flowed from his eyes. He tried again and still couldn't. All he could do was shake hands and embrace old friends.[25]

6

Cabinet Making

With four months until his March 4, 1921, inauguration, the first task of President-elect Harding was to select a cabinet, which he envisioned as a foundation of his presidency. During the campaign, Harding had declared, "I should not be fit to hold the high office of President if I did not frankly say that it is a task which I have no intention of undertaking alone." He planned to seek the advice of "the best minds in the United States."[1]

Few men have entered the presidency with less baggage than Harding. He had made no deals and owed no one any favors or patronage, particularly in the U.S. Senate. Nor did he need to rush any decisions. Accordingly, the day after his landslide victory, he announced that he was going to take a vacation. He urged newspapers not to speculate on his cabinet selections because he had made no decisions and did not plan to do so until he returned to Marion. Of course, the press immediately began filling its pages with intense speculation. For example, the New York Times reported (incorrectly) that both General Wood and Governor Lowden were going to be part of Harding's cabinet.

First Harding traveled to Texas, where he spent several days with Frank Scobey, fishing and playing golf and poker. He asked the press for some privacy. Harding explained that he felt it important that whoever was president should exercise regularly and he didn't climb mountains like TR; rather, like Woodrow Wilson, he was a golfer. But since he was such a lousy golfer he would rather not have to read about it in the newspapers. Harding's Secret Service agent reported that "[n]o matter how bad his lie, he played it, even when his opponents begged him to pick it up."[2] Reporters agreed to give him his privacy but they wanted to know how to deal with the situation of his doing something newsworthy while playing golf. Harding answered that if he broke 100 they could report it, for that would be real news and he wouldn't mind reading about it.

After Texas, the Hardings took a cruise to Panama. The cruise ended back in Norfolk, Virginia, on December 4, 1920, and the Hardings proceeded to Washington for the third session of the 66th Congress. It was an emotional visit when they returned to the Senate on December 6. Soon-to-be–first lady Florence Harding, accompanied by her friend Evalyn Walsh McLean, attended a luncheon of Senate wives arranged by Vice President Marshall's wife. When Florence entered the luncheon she was stunned to receive a standing ovation. During her many years of attending affairs with other Senate wives she had been made to feel an unimportant outsider. It was a satisfying and happy moment for her. Equally emotional was Warren Harding's return. When he swept into the Senate chamber through the doors of the Republican cloakroom, all his colleagues rose to applaud, as did the packed gallery when he walked to his Senate desk. Senator Lodge, the Republican leader, was recognized by Vice President Marshall, who was presiding. Lodge, noting that this was the first time an active member of the Senate had been elected president, requested that Harding be given permission to address his colleagues from the chair. Applause again broke out and the vice president stepped down as Harding mounted the dais. There, in a heartfelt speech, he talked of his regret in leaving his colleagues. But the subtext of his remarks and his demeanor held another message. Since his election victory the newspapers had talked endlessly about the Senate cabal that had selected Harding and now was controlling the president-elect. Without any direct reference to this media blather, Harding's talk to his colleagues made clear that he was his own man and he answered not to the U.S. Senate but rather to the American people.

Two messages for Florence soon arrived at Harding's Senate office: Alice Roosevelt Longworth wanted to speak with them both and Florence was invited by First Lady Edith Wilson to tea, at 4 P.M. the next day, December 7, so she could see the White House to make arrangements for their move.

Alice Longworth, who had early called Harding a crooked politician and was not one to be among the outs when her party was in, had mended her fence with Harding as soon as he was nominated at the convention. In Chicago, they talked about what had happened in 1912 and, according to Alice, "agreed that we both should try to forget the details of that bitter year." She also reported on her meeting with Harding after his visit with the Senate, which appears to have included her husband, Ohio congressman Nick Longworth, where they tried to get Harding to exclude Harry Daugherty from a cabinet post.[3]

The White House tea was not a pleasant experience for Florence. Edith Wilson was haughty, even condescending, and later wrote of an obviously nervous and excited Florence: "Her manner was so effusive, so voluble, that after a half-hour over the tea cups I could hardly stem the torrent of words." Rather than show her about the executive mansion, Edith Wilson called for the housekeeper, Mrs. Elizabeth Jaffray, to give Florence a tour; claiming another appointment, Edith promptly disappeared. During this tour, Florence discovered she was in the home of a sick man, and decided that as soon as they moved in she would open up, and cheer up, the White House. A few hours later Edith Wilson returned and "heard a voice far down in the kitchen. It was Mrs. Harding talking to the cook.

She remained until after eight o'clock," Mrs. Wilson complained. Florence, not wanting to pick a fight with Edith Wilson, told reporters she had a very pleasant visit.[4]

Back home in Marion, the Hardings' house once again became the focus of national attention. A steady stream of éminences grises arrived to confer with Harding and assist with his search for the best minds for his cabinet. Advice poured in and Harding listened patiently and asked questions. He also consulted from time to time with his running mate, Calvin Coolidge, but, as in the campaign, Coolidge's role was minimal. And Florence Harding had no hesitation about tossing in her thoughts as well. Harding explained he was considering three factors in making his selections: "First, there is the man's qualifications for public service. That is the most important consideration of all. Second, there is the attitude of the public concerning the man under consideration. Third, there is the political consideration. As to that—well. This is going to be a Republican Cabinet."

By tradition, and because of its importance, the first post to be filled was that of secretary of state. Henry Cabot Lodge, as an elder of the party and chairman of the Senate Foreign Relations Committee, felt he should have a voice in this selection and proffered endless advice to the president-elect, no doubt hoping Harding might select Lodge himself. Lodge was never an option in Harding's eyes, nor were Lodge's preferences of former senator and former secretary of state as well as the 1912 Nobel Peace laureate Elihu Root, nor Senator Philander Knox, former attorney general and former secretary of state. Although both men were obviously qualified, Harding felt both were a bit older than he wished.

Harding briefly considered Albert Fall for secretary of state, principally because Fall had been strongly recommended by the man who Harding wanted for the job, Charles Evans Hughes.[5] Hughes, who was a vigorous fifty-nine years of age, was ideal. Although not the man the conservative Republicans favored, as the party's 1916 standard-bearer he was the logical choice for the top cabinet post. His educational background and record of public service were impeccable. He was a former governor of New York and associate justice of the U.S. Supreme Court, not to mention a skilled lawyer and able negotiator. When Hughes informed Harding he could not accept the post because of a potential conflict of interest with a client, it gave Lodge and other conservative Republicans an opportunity to try to change Harding's mind, claiming Hughes lacked experience in foreign affairs. But Harding refused to budge, and Hughes's conflict was resolved.

At the State Department Harding also wanted to select the undersecretary of state. During his Senate years Harding worked with Henry P. Fletcher, who once was one of TR's Rough Riders and had held a number of diplomatic posts including ambassador to Mexico in 1916. Harding wanted to make Fletcher undersecretary to assist him in making ambassadorial appointments, and once that was completed, Fletcher hoped to be an ambassador himself. No doubt this is why Hughes did not complain. And in fact, that is precisely the way it worked out. By December 1921 the ambassadorial appointments, for all practical purposes, had been completed and Fletcher was hoping for one of the posts he dearly wanted. Fletcher was surprised, however, by how he learned of his new appointment.

During the ten months Fletcher served as undersecretary, Harding regularly sent what became an almost standardized letter of inquiry. Such a letter from the president arrived in Fletcher's mail on December 24, 1921: "I wish you would direct an inquiry to the Belgium Government about the acceptability of Henry Prather Fletcher, of Pennsylvania, whom I have in mind as a possible nominee to the Ambassadorship to that country. I do not know if you will wholly approve of this nomination, but I have promised some insistent political friends that I would make it and I must, therefore, trouble you to address the usual inquiry to the Belgium Government." A delighted

Fletcher wrote back: "It is a rare, but very pleasant thing, to find an Embassy in your Christmas stocking."[6]

The nation's economy in the aftermath of the war was not good. It was experiencing deflation, credit was tight, and domestic markets were glutted with heavy inventories, accompanied by a sharp drop in foreign trade.[7] Postwar European agriculture had recovered quickly and at the expense of American farmers. Throughout the 1920 campaign Harding had consulted with Henry C. Wallace about the plight of farmers. Wallace, who grew up on a dirt farm and became a professor of agriculture at Iowa State University, was the outspoken editor of *Wallace's Farmer,* a popular farm journal that he and his father edited. A few days before the election Harding sent Wallace a note, telling him, "If the verdict of Tuesday is what we are expecting it to be I shall very much want your assistance in making good the promises which we have made to the American people."[8] In December, Harding asked Wallace to be his secretary of agriculture. Harding knew he would have to take political flack for selecting Wallace, because his liberal leanings were offensive to the right wing of the party, but the president-elect understood that the party's progressives would embrace and support Wallace.*

Harding's first choice to run the Department of the Treasury was Charles G. Dawes, head of the Central Union Trust Company of Illinois. Dawes had grown up in Ohio, studied law, and launched his career litigating against unfair rail rates. Harding probably first met Dawes during McKinley's 1896 presidential campaign, when Dawes was the Illinois manager. After the election McKinley asked Dawes to come to Washington to serve as comptroller of the currency. During World War I Dawes served as major in the engineering corps, where General John J. Pershing spotted the former official. General Pershing made Dawes the

---

* Henry C. Wallace's son, Henry A. Wallace, would serve as President Franklin Roosevelt's secretary of agriculture and later vice president.

general purchasing agent of the American Expeditionary Forces in France, where Dawes skillfully supplied the army's needs while eliminating waste and holding prices down. This was the reason Harding asked Dawes to serve as secretary of the Treasury.

Dawes was hesitant, telling Harding that there was little the secretary of the Treasury could do to cut government spending and trim the federal budget, as Harding had pledged to do. The Treasury secretary had limited powers over federal expenditures, and Dawes knew that other cabinet officers would resent his efforts to control their expenditures. Dawes and Harding discussed what could, however, be done to cut the budget. President Wilson had vetoed legislation to create a Bureau of the Budget with a budget director who reported directly to the president. By getting Congress to again pass this law, Harding could trim the budget and eliminate the existing system where each department and agency went to Congress to get what it could, with the White House having no real controls. Harding placed the new budget legislation at the top of his priority list and got a commitment from Dawes that he would head the budget unit after it became law.

Dawes's reluctance to take the post of secretary of the Treasury proved fortuitous in not only making him available to later be the first director of the Bureau of the Budget, but the Treasury post enabled Harding to do a bit of horse trading in assembling his cabinet. Harding kept testing the name of Herbert Hoover, as he met with those interested in his selections. Harding liked Hoover and had met him when Woodrow Wilson brought him to Washington at the outbreak of World War I to head the Food Administration. After the armistice, Hoover headed the American Relief Administration, which provided food for millions starving in central Europe. Harding was impressed with young Hoover and wanted him in his cabinet, but Republican elders and conservatives objected. For example, Hoover's critics charged him with helping Bolshevism by extending American aid to famine-stricken Russia.

Hoover defiantly retorted, "Twenty million people are starving. Whatever their politics, they shall be fed!"

Harding experienced more internal party squabbling and opposition to Hoover than any of his choices. Notwithstanding old-guard opposition that he was too liberal, too ambitious, too international in his views, not to mention too publicly popular, Harding offered Hoover the Department of Commerce or the Department of Interior. Hoover picked Commerce. Leading the effort to block Hoover was the ailing Pennsylvania senator Boies Penrose, who was being supported by an increasingly meddlesome Henry Cabot Lodge. When Penrose, backed by Lodge, began pushing Pittsburgh billionaire financier Andrew Mellon for secretary of the Treasury, Harding saw an opportunity. Harding knew and greatly admired Mellon, and thought him potentially a great Treasury secretary. But rather than express delight to have Mellon at Treasury, he agreed only to consider Mellon. Harding was about to show his skill as a politician.

For Treasury, Harding wanted a man who was acceptable to Wall Street, but was not a product of Wall Street. Mellon fit perfectly. Soon the second-richest man in the country (just behind John D. Rockefeller) arrived in Marion for his meeting with the president-elect. The two men agreed that the country needed a prompt and thorough revision of the tax system, emergency tariffs, readjustment of war taxes, and creation of a federal budget system, among other economic measures. This titan of business had never held public office, so he told Harding that he didn't think he would make a very good secretary of the Treasury. But Mellon didn't say "no" and Harding urged him to keep an open mind.

Following Mellon's visit, word of his possibly of going to Treasury spread fast, with financial journals declaring Mellon potentially the greatest secretary of the Treasury since Alexander Hamilton. Harding saw an opportunity both to get Mellon and to solve his problem with Herbert Hoover. So Harding dispatched Harry Daugherty to personally give Penrose and Lodge a message:

"Mellon and Hoover or no Mellon."[9] They agreed to stop carping about Hoover. Harding was delighted when Mellon accepted. Harding biographer Andrew Sinclair writes, "Harding shared in the popular American belief that a few great international figures controlled the economic destiny of the world. The thing was to employ one of them in the service of the nation, and the result would be prosperity for all and not merely himself. . . . [Harding] termed Mellon 'the ubiquitous financier of the universe' and considered his appointment to the Cabinet a stroke of good fortune."[10] Mellon did prove to be a great Treasury secretary, serving in the post not only during the Harding administration but during Coolidge's and Hoover's as well.

In backing the Mellon selection, Henry Cabot Lodge was trying to ride two horses simultaneously. Lodge supported Penrose's push for Mellon with the understanding of Harding and Penrose that former Massachusetts senator John Weeks was to be given a cabinet post. Harding's first thought was to make Weeks the secretary of the navy, given his naval background. But Weeks was reluctant because that job might require him to pass judgment on many of his Annapolis classmates. But there was also the Department of War. There was much public and editorial support for Harding to select General Leonard Wood to head the War Department.[11] But Wood had left old wounds with Harding untended and the president-elect was reluctant to place the still politically ambitious Wood in his cabinet.[12] Harding thought John Weeks ideal for the War Department. He had served in the navy and was on the Board of Visitors of the Naval Academy; after eight years in the U.S. House of Representatives, he spent twelve years in the U.S. Senate. In a meeting with Harding in Marion on January 15, 1921, John Weeks agreed to become secretary of war, where he proved a popular choice with the Congress and the services.*

---

* John Weeks's son, Sinclair Weeks, served as President Dwight Eisenhower's secretary of commerce.

Filling the top job at the Department of Labor was delicate for the pro-business Republican administration. The economy was in bad shape, with unemployment figures reaching record highs in late 1920 and early 1921. Nonfarm unemployment had gone from 2.3 percent in 1919 to 4.0 percent in 1920, but soared to 11.9 percent in 1921.[13] Labor strife was frequently erupting into violent disturbances. The powerful American Federation of Labor president, Samuel Gompers, had aggressively opposed Harding, earning a degree of enmity from the president-elect. Harding directed his search team to find someone from the ranks of labor who was anti-Gompers, yet acceptable to both labor and business. The Labor Department at this time also handled immigration, and as the economy had turned down, concern about immigrants taking jobs increased. Immigration politics added another dimension to the responsibilities of the labor secretary, and Harding's search produced a uniquely qualified candidate: James J. ("Puddler Jim") Davis.

Born in Wales, Jim Davis immigrated to Pennsylvania at eight years of age and went straight to work in a steel mill as a puddler's assistant—thus his nickname. By the time Harding recruited him he was a successful and wealthy banker, an exemplar of the American dream. Yet he remained an active member of the Amalgamated Association of Iron, Steel, and Tin Workers. He had credentials to deal with not only labor problems but immigration as well, given his background. Word leaked of who Harding was considering for the labor job and Gompers telegraphed the president-elect to protest, which sealed Harding's decision. Harding telegraphed Davis to come to Marion on January 7, and three days later Davis was there and accepted the post. As the director-general of the fraternal organization Loyal Order of the Moose, lodges everywhere came to his support, as did many labor organizations. Davis would distinguish himself as an outstanding labor secretary, who strengthened the Labor Department's reporting of labor information, encouraged labor-management cooperation, and, with Harding's backing, persuaded U.S. Steel to abolish the twelve-hour workday. Davis served three presidents, Harding, Coolidge, and Hoover, before being elected to the U.S. Senate, where he authored the landmark Davis-Beacon Act (requiring contractors on federal jobs to pay workers no less than the wages prevailing in the local area).[14]

No one was surprised when Harding selected Will Hays as postmaster general for it was a post where presidents often placed their party chairman. Hays had wanted the Department of Commerce but it had been promised to Hoover, and there is no indication Harding considered Hays for any other job. Former president Taft had advised Harding that Hays was a lightweight, and, indeed, he did not enjoy great success in running the post office. His tenure as postmaster was plagued by mail robberies, which became so troublesome Hays raised the problem with Harding's cabinet, which resulted in a decision to dispatch a thousand marines to protect the mail. This worked and cut theft losses from $6 million to a mere $300,000.[15] Unlike many in the Harding cabinet, Hays was not a wealthy man, and after he had been postmaster only a year he received a job offer that he could not refuse: the head of the Motion Picture Producers and Distributors of America, with a salary of $150,000 a year (a remarkable sum at the time).

Harding continued meeting with advisers in Marion about the cabinet, and he began working on his inauguration speech, as well as programs he planned to recommend to Congress. Harding decided to approach Frank Lowden to ask if he was interested in being the secretary of navy, as a way to thank Lowden and his constituents for their support during the convention and the campaign. The offer was conveyed on January 17, 1921. Lowden assumed it was being tendered as a mere courtesy but, in fact, Harding was serious and assured Lowden that was the case. Because Harding was interested in having Lowden join the cabinet, he told Lowden he was going to Florida for about a month to complete his preinauguration work, and said he would give Lowden until mid-February to consider.

There were ten cabinet posts in 1921. Before going to Florida Harding had resolved his selections for seven of the departments: State, Treasury, War, Agriculture, Labor, Post Office, and Commerce. Remaining were the Interior, Justice, and Navy departments. When Albert Fall and Harry Daugherty joined Harding in Florida, speculation correctly assumed that Fall might be offered the Department of Interior and Daugherty the Justice Department. Many words, and much ink, would be devoted to these two men because of the murky shadows they later cast on the Harding presidency. Harding biographer Robert Murray explains, however, that the story of their selection was rather simple: Harding's "friendship for Albert Fall and his gratitude to Harry Daugherty" were what placed them high on his list and soon in his cabinet.

Fall was certainly qualified to head the Interior Department, which traditionally was headed by a Westerner. Interior's principal concern was with the nation's public lands and natural resources. Fall had spent his life in mining, ranching, and oil. Throughout the 1920 campaign, and during the post-election cabinet-making process, Harding consulted with Fall, who had planned to leave the Senate to return to private practice. Fall was not looking for a job in Harding's cabinet, yet every time he and Harding met following the election, Harding insisted Fall should be one of his cabinet officers. As Fall explained to his wife: "He [Harding] thinks that the Interior Department is second only to the State Department in importance and that there is more opportunity for graft and scandal connected with the disposition of public lands &c, than there could be in other Departments and he wants a man who is thoroughly honest, etc., etc."[16] Harding critics later claimed that putting Fall in Interior was like putting a bank robber in a bank. In fact, it appears Harding thought he was doing precisely the opposite. Fall's biographer reports that "[h]e agonized for three days and finally accepted."

Daugherty's possible selection to be attorney general was highly controversial. On February 11, 1921, the *New York Times* editorially advised against it: "If Mr. Harding has any close and trusted advisers who are not afraid to tell him the truth, even if it be unwelcome, they ought to lay before him in the plainest way the blunder he would make if he chose Mr. Daugherty as his Attorney General." The *Times* minced no words in explaining its thinking: "It would be universally regarded as the payment of a political debt. But it would be worse than that. It would be the naming of a man not believed to be competent to do the important work to be placed in his hands. . . . It will be better for Mr. Harding's friends to tell him bluntly in advance what a bad impression would be made by appointing Mr. Daugherty Attorney General than to wait until after the mischief is done."

No reporter was harder on Daugherty than Louis Seibold, a correspondent for the *New York World* who could not find enough nasty things to say about the Columbus attorney so he simply speculated as to how awful he might be as attorney general. Seibold's criticism finally got to Harding. Journalist Samuel Hopkins Adams recounted the incident. Harding had been holding daily press conferences in Florida, and Seibold showed up for the press briefing on February 21. "Although he [Harding] liked Seibold and continued to like him, Harding's face flushed at the sight of him. There was a challenge in his manner as he announced his choice for the Department of Justice, 'Harry M. Daugherty, a splendid man, an able man, and he will make a great Attorney General.' Pointedly addressing [Seibold] in the phraseology of their common craft, he rasped: 'And you can set that up in block on the front page of your paper.'"[17]

Later that evening, Adams reports, Daugherty ran into Seibold. "Louis," Daugherty said pleasantly (for he was not one to hold grudges), "that was a great favor you did me today." Seibold was confused, "How is that?" Daugherty continued, "I've been trying to get Harding to make up his mind about me. He kept sidestepping. Now he's named me and it was seeing you there that did the trick. I owe you one for that." Daugherty was not being facetious and to prove it he gave Seibold a solid tip for the last open slot on the cabinet, Edwin N. Denby to be secretary of the navy.

Frank Lowden had turned down Navy, and Harding's recruiters recommended former three-term Michigan congressman Edward Denby, who signed up for the marines in World War I before he was eighteen, and completed his active duty as a major. A lawyer by training, he turned to business after the war, making himself a millionaire in the automotive industry. A devoted public servant throughout his successful business career, he had been a voluntary probation officer with the Detroit Municipal Court. Harding gave little thought to this post, and Denby was not much of a navy secretary.

Well before his inauguration, Harding arranged for the names of his cabinet to be quietly submitted to the Senate. Republican Senate leader Lodge cleared all the names with all the committees before Harding's swearing-in, so that after his inauguration address he could personally submit his cabinet to the Senate and have it approved. This plan was known to only a handful in the Senate. Harding had resigned his Senate seat on January 6, 1921, waiting until Governor Cox (who he defeated for president) had been replaced by his Republican successor, who had been elected on Harding's coattails. Former governor Frank Willis, who had won Harding's seat, was appointed to fill the remaining time of Harding's term, thereby giving him seniority over other senators elected in 1920, which was good for Willis and Ohio given the importance of seniority in the Senate.

When Harding dropped by the Senate chamber less than an hour after his inauguration address, it was a dramatic moment. Former members of the Senate are given the special privilege of returning to the Senate floor, at any time, so Harding needed no permission (as had Woodrow Wilson) when he visited the Senate chamber. With Vice President Calvin Coolidge in his new seat as the presiding officer of the Senate, in an executive session (closed to the public and press) Harding read the list of his cabinet nominees. Knowing the reaction it would cause when he named Albert Fall as secretary of interior, he named Fall first, which brought Fall's colleagues to their feet. Fall was the first (and last) cabinet officer to be confirmed by instant acclamation of the Senate. The new president then continued: secretary of state—Charles E. Hughes, secretary of the Treasury—Andrew W. Mellon, secretary of war—John W. Weeks, attorney general—Harry M. Daugherty, postmaster general—Will H. Hays, secretary of the navy—Edwin N. Denby, secretary of agriculture—Henry C. Wallace, secretary of commerce—Herbert C. Hoover, and secretary of labor—James J. Davis. The entire cabinet was confirmed without objection in record time, less than ten minutes.[18]

It was a carefully crafted, well-built cabinet, composed of distinguished, self-made men of independent public standing. It was a cabinet with a future president (Hoover), a future chief justice (Hughes), and a future felon (Fall). With the exception of Fall, none of Harding's appointees had ties to the public constituency served by their departments nor a preexisting relationship with the bureaucracy within those departments. In short, none was a specialist. Presidents who fill cabinet posts with such men (and later women)—persons with the recognized skills of the "generalist executive"—as Harding did, are typically given high marks.[19] In Harding's case that did not happen. History has focused on Fall. Yet at the time Harding's cabinet was announced, Fall was highly praised, as were all but Daugherty. After Harding's death, his able team was labeled by many as mere "deodorizers." But not even Madame Marcia could have foretold the fate that later came to pass with Albert Fall, a bad apple Harding's detractors have used to suggest a wider rot than in truth existed. Appraising Harding's cabinet when it was formed, the *New York Times* spoke of its "high caliber" and "a guarantee of success," and the *Atlantic Monthly*, assessing the cabinet after its first two years, found that "No presidential cabinet during the past half-century has been better balanced, or has included within its membership a wider range of political experience."[20] It was not a cabinet of a weak or inept president, and no president before or after Harding has done any better at cabinet making.

7

An Unfinished Presidency

Harding entered office at a time when the United States was adrift. The ship of state had been floating aimlessly if not dangerously without a captain. For seventeen months President Wilson had been ill, and even before his debilitating stroke he had spent many months out of the country (and largely out of touch), trying to negotiate the settlement of the world war. Harding biographer Robert Murray succinctly states the situation facing Harding: "From Wilson he received a disintegrating presidency, a confused and rebellious Congress, a foreign policy in chaos, a domestic economy in shambles, a society sundered with hatreds and turmoil."[1] Or as Edmund W. Starling, chief of the White House Secret Service and an admirer of Wilson, summed it up best: "the country was in a mess."[2] A shattered and sickly Wilson had to be lifted into the open automobile that drove the president and president-elect to the Capitol for the Harding inauguration ceremony, and Wilson was not even strong enough to remain for the swearing-in.

On March 4, 1921, Harding came to the inaugural podium bareheaded, tanned, strikingly presidential in appearance with his gray hair and commanding physical presence. His inaugural address was the first ever to be electronically amplified for the assembled crowd, as well as broadcast via radio throughout the country and around the world.

"My Countrymen. When one surveys the world about him after the great storm," he began, turning first to the role of the United States as a member of the world community, and making clear his belief that America should have "no part in directing the destinies of the Old World. We do not mean to be entangled." Yet he assured other nations that the United States would never turn its back on humankind, should it be necessary to take military action again. His point was clear: his administration would not participate in the League of Nations but America would remain vigilant and prepared to assist others as necessary. On behalf of a grateful nation he made a point of thanking "the maimed and wounded soldiers who are present." Then he turned to the nation's "supreme task," which he described as "the resumption of our onward, normal ways. Reconstruction, readjustment, restoration—all these must follow. I would like to hasten them." He criticized businesses that had excessively profited from the war while others were fighting, and he made clear that the troubled economy was at the top of his agenda: "We can reduce the abnormal expenditures, and we will. We can strike at war taxation, and we must. . . . Our most dangerous tendency is to expect too much of government, and at the same time do for it too little." Harding's address, like those of presidents who preceded and followed, set the tone for his presidency and highlighted his priorities.

Holding down inaugural expenses and opening the White House grounds for the first time in eight years won widespread public and press approval, as did the president's getting right down to business. His second day at the White House, a Saturday, commenced early when he arrived in the Oval Office to gather his thoughts and make notes for a meeting with congressional leaders. Speaker of the House Frederick H. Gillette from Massachusetts and Senator Henry Cabot Lodge, also from Massachusetts, headed the visiting Capitol Hill delegation. For the first time in ten years Republicans controlled both legislative and executive branches. Harding's coattails had given Republicans an overwhelming majority in the 67th Congress.[3] In contrast to Wilson, who had frequently tried to badger the Congress into adopting his programs, only to have Congress revolt, Harding had vowed to offer Congress his best advice and let the legislative branch work its will.[4] For the first two years of his presidency he kept this promise. Accordingly, at the outset of his term he asked the Republican leaders of Congress for their priorities. While he discovered that there was no clear consensus, two matters emerged from his meeting as more important than others: tax reform and emergency tariffs. And it was agreed that the president should call a special session of Congress to deal with these and other pending problems.*

On March 8, 1921, Harding held his first cabinet meeting, telling his appointees that, unlike Wilson, he wanted and expected their advice and counsel. He planned to convene the cabinet at 10 A.M. every Tuesday and Friday and ask that cabinet members come prepared to report on issues and matters of importance before their departments. The president laid out the rules for the cabinet: no one other than members of the cabinet would attend their meetings, no secretary would record their discussions, and no record would be kept of any of their votes because he wanted outspoken advice freely given without concern about making a record. Cabinet meetings were to be confidential, with only the president having the privilege of revealing their discussions and decisions.[5] When this first meeting turned to substantive matters, Harding found his cabinet had no clearer thoughts on legislative priorities than did the congressional leaders. Harding requested that each cabinet officer make accommodations for the newsmen at their respective departments.[6] And he told the cabinet that he planned to meet with newsmen himself after cabinet meetings.

---

* The 66th Congress expired on March 4, 1921; the 67th Congress (those elected with Harding in November 1920) was not due to convene until the first Monday in December 1921. Thus the special session assembled the new Congress nine months early.

Another precedent Harding set was to make his vice president a member of his cabinet. This decision later resulted in a nearly seamless transition of power following Harding's death.

Harding appreciated that not only to govern effectively, but to get reelected, he needed the press. On March 21, 1921, he held his first presidential press conference, with about fifty reporters. In fact, he met them at the door of the Oval Office, shaking hands with each, adding personal greetings or words for those he knew. He then went back to his desk, where he stood and answered their questions. One reason reporters liked Harding was explained by another reporter who covered Harding's administration: "Harding talked freely about the operations of government," Frederick Essary said.[7] Harding was known by reporters for his openness and frankness.

As Harding's White House press conferences evolved, guidelines were adopted. Unfortunately for history, no stenographic record was made because Harding wanted to keep them informal. Unless the president indicated otherwise, he was not to be directly quoted; rather, he was referred to as "a high official" or some such similar identification. After eight months' experience, and when the numbers attending had significantly grown, Harding added another rule to increase the efficiency of the sessions. With increasing numbers of reporters attending, often many reporters did not get answers to their questions that both they and the president felt were important. Accordingly, the White House created a question box, where reporters deposited their questions up to the time of the press conference. Then, at the press conference, the written questions were given to the president and he would decide which he should and would answer as well as those he felt—as a matter of policy—he should not answer. As the *New York Times* explained, "at times conflicting interpretations have been placed on his refusal to answer." Given the range of questions asked, which the *Times* described as "from cabbages to kings," his occasional failure to respond as fully as the reporter or editor might have liked had on occasion been "misconstrued." The written-question arrangement solved this problem and pleased both reporters and their editors.

It is often incorrectly reported that Harding instituted the written-question practice after he made a misstatement (that had been quickly corrected) during the Washington Disarmament Conference in late December 1921, and because of his misstatement, Secretary of State Hughes had demanded that Harding institute the written procedure. This explanation is not correct; had those who concocted the story (or those who have often repeated it) bothered to check, they would have learned that the *New York Times* of December 21, 1921, reported that the president had misspoken during the Disarmament Conference "in response to a written question," for the procedure had been implemented a month earlier, which was also reported in the *Times*.[8]

Naturally, neither Harding nor the White House press corps was always completely happy with their relationship. A president always has more information than can be given to the news media; and the news media always wants more from a president than can be given. Even so, Harding's unique relationship with the news media continued. Harding biographer Robert Murray, writing in 1969, found that "[u]nquestionably Harding had the best relationship with the press of any president in history." To Murray's statement it might be added, "while he was alive." With the exception of the early years of FDR, no president has ever had the open and comfortable relationship with reporters that Harding did. As Murray explains, Harding's "affinity [with the working press] arose partially from the fact that he, too, was a newspaper man. But it went beyond that. Reporters liked his frankness in confessing his limitations and his refreshing candor about presidential problems. The press was taken behind the scenes and shown the inner workings of the presidency to an extent never allowed before."[9] However, it should not be assumed that this relationship caused the press to cover for him later, when the going got tough.

Even though Harding was responsible for the overwhelming Republican majority in Congress, he did not enjoy the traditional congressional honeymoon. To the contrary, the U.S. Senate kept testing him, only to find him firm and unwavering. On April 12, 1921, Harding addressed a joint session of Congress concerning the policies, plans, and matters he believed the Congress should undertake. To the surprise of many, and the delight of more, the president set forth in considerable detail the laws he believed were needed and why. It was a lengthy and comprehensive speech seeking to stimulate action by drawing public attention to his recommendations. He found a receptive audience. In the hour it required to deliver, he was interrupted by applause on thirty occasions. The speech was not a Wilsonian lecture but a clear, and rather blunt, delineation of what needed to be done, both immediately and in the near term. He was defining his policy of normalcy but, unlike his inaugural address or campaign oratory, it contained few political platitudes. Harding's normalcy was not a call to turn back the clock (as many have written), but rather, as he had earlier stated in his inaugural (although few had heard) and again in opening his address to Congress, he was calling for "*onward*, normal ways."

Harding's message to Congress "showed that he possessed an awareness of every major problem confronting the nation even though he did not have a solution for each one."[10] But he had many answers and he gave them to Congress. The message focused on domestic problems, yet he urged Congress to make a formal peace with Germany and Austria by a joint resolution, since technically the nation remained at war. The economy was his priority. He called on Congress to cut government expenditures by creating a Bureau of the Budget, he urged revising the federal tax laws including the abolition of the excess profits tax, and he requested that Congress enact emergency tariffs followed in six months with more comprehensive revisions. He spoke frankly of agriculture's problems (acknowledging that tariffs were only part of a solution); he called for a new immigration law; he raised the need to deal with emerging transportation problems (railroads, highways, as well as the new civil and military aviation); he asked Congress to regulate the new technology of radio and transcontinental cable communications; and he called for establishing a stronger merchant marine. No request surprised and confounded his conservative colleagues more than his recommendation that they create a department of public welfare that would be responsible for "education, public health, sanitation, conditions of workers in industry, child welfare, proper amusement and recreation, the elimination of social vices." Notwithstanding Harding's conservative thinking, his nature could never ignore the wellbeing of his fellow man. After eight years of ignoring the problems of race, Harding faced "the race question" directly. "Congress ought to wipe the stain of barbaric lynching from the banners of a free and orderly, representative democracy," he declared.[11]

Congress quickly passed a new immigration law and sent it to Harding. Nativism, that ugly sister of nationalism, had emerged in the aftermath of the war. Foreigners were suspect and unwanted. The fact that they were taking jobs during a time of serious unemployment aggravated the nation's nativistic mood and produced almost universal support—from organized labor to big business, including both liberal and conservative journals—for restricting immigration. For the special session of Congress it was only a question of how severe the restriction needed to be. Congressman Albert Johnson, a Washington state Republican chairman of the House Immigration Committee, wanted a total ban on all immigration but had failed to get it during the prior 66th Congress, when the Senate balked by cutting immigration quotas to only 3 percent of any given country's nationals residing in the United States as of 1910. President Wilson had defeated the 3 percent bill

with a pocket veto (letting it die on his desk without signing it).
No sooner had Harding's special session opened than the House
passed with a voice vote the identical bill Wilson had killed. The
Senate in turn approved the bill 78 to 1 and sent it to the White
House. Harding signed the Per Centum Act, making it law on
May 19, 1921.

Enforcement of this harsh new law fell to the secretary of labor,
James Davis, who, it will be recalled, was himself an immigrant.
Calls for the law had caused a rush of new arrivals in the United
States, and when the law was enacted sooner than anyone
expected, it resulted in many immigrants finding themselves outside the quotas effective as of June 1921. Secretary Davis carried
the hardship cases to the president, and to the displeasure of strict
restrictionists, Harding frequently made exceptions, saving almost
a thousand immigrants from deportation. Harding and Davis both
believed the law was necessary but thought its enforcement had
to be humane. To facilitate enforcement of the law, Harding also
created a new post of assistant secretary of labor for immigration,
and he sent a well-known lawyer and labor expert, Meyer Bloom-
field, to Europe to develop screening centers to prevent people
from traveling to the United States only to find themselves turned
away under the new law. While Harding was criticized for his
compassion, opponents could bark only so loud when the law was,
in fact, being fully enforced—only Harding and Davis were doing
so wisely. Not until 1924, after Harding's death, did the Congress
deal further with the "temporary" immigration measure.

On May 27, 1921, Harding signed his second law, an emergency tariff statute on select foreign imports. This stopgap measure had easily passed both the House and Senate because farmers
and industry were calling for it. Europe's rapid agricultural recovery had been at the expense of American farmers, who had profited handsomely during the war. Congress also tacked on to the
emergency tariff bill the antidumping provisions (tariffs prevent-
ing the sale of imports at low prices) requested by American man-

ufacturers. But this quick-fix measure did little to solve the problems facing American agriculture or to satisfy postwar American
industries that were being forced to compete with the rest of the
world. Tariff questions demanded much attention of the new
president and remained an issue throughout his tenure.

In dealing with tariffs, Harding showed his ability to grow in
office. He quickly learned that the simplistic tariff remedies he had
preached in his *Star* editorials and as a candidate were not so practical after all. He entered office believing in the Republican policy
of high tariffs but discovered that tariffs have their own price. The
world had changed since 1909 when his party had hiked rates in
the Payne-Aldrich Tariff law. By 1921, tariff protection as a means
of dealing with foreign competition had different consequences,
for the United States was no longer a debtor nation. Rather the
United States had become the world's chief creditor and its economy relied greatly on its exports. Harding realized that tariff pro-
tectionism was a potentially dangerous game.

By July 1921 the House passed a bill that increased tariffs across
the board. Encouraging such action was federal tariff commissioner
Thomas Marvin, who had his own thoughts on tariffs. The Senate,
busy with other matters, did not take up the House bill and the
delay gave other members of the Federal Tariff Commission an
opportunity to speak out in disagreement with Commissioner
Marvin. In fact, Marvin's view was not shared by his colleagues,
and the consensus of the Tariff Commission was that the Congress
needed to act with caution. Enacting permanent tariffs so quickly
after the war would invite trouble. Not only was American manufacturing in a state of fluctuation; so, too, were the values of various
European currencies. The concern of the majority of the Tariff
Commission did not go unheard at the White House.

President Harding, who had in fact instinctively believed Commissioner Marvin was right, was now becoming educated and having second thoughts. Not an economist, and having little more
knowledge of the field than reading Adam Smith's *Wealth of*

Nations, Harding turned to tariff commissioner William S. Culbertson, a lawyer with a Ph.D. in economics from Yale, who Wilson had appointed to the Federal Tariff Commission.[12] Harding's papers contain a number of lengthy memoranda from Culbertson to Harding in which Culbertson was tutoring the president. Culbertson, who was a mild protectionist, advised Harding that what was needed at that time was maximum flexibility, given the fluid domestic and international situation. "As a result of his exposure to [Culbertson's] arguments, Harding became much more sophisticated in his own thinking on the tariff [issue] between election day and late 1921," Dr. Murray found, noting that while Harding retained his protectionist bias, "he came to realize that an intelligent tariff policy could not be capricious or arbitrary and that it had to take into account a complicated variety of other domestic and international economic factors."[13]

In his December 6, 1921, state of the union address, Harding showed his new understanding of tariffs by calling attention to the need for flexibility. Not until April 11, 1922, did the Senate finally go to work on a tariff bill, the Fordney-McCumber Act, named after its protectionist sponsors Joesph W. Fordney, chairman of the House Ways and Means Committee, and Senator Porter J. McCumber, chairman of the Senate Finance Committee. The Senate spent the next four months haggling over the bill, finally passing it on August 19, and then the House and Senate spent another month quarreling over their differences before finding compromise and sending it to the White House. Only one group could have benefited from the Senate bill—the Washington lobbyists, who were out in force representing the conflicting and competing special interests. The final bill was a hodgepodge of conciliations with each special interest happy with its own protection but unhappy with any protection given to others. When Harding signed the bill on September 21, 1922, he was less than exuberant, offering an unusually brief statement after giving the gold-plated pen with which he signed the law to Joe Fordney:

"Thank you for coming, gentlemen. This law has been long in the making. I don't know how many are in accord with me, but if we succeed in making effective the elastic provisions of the measure it will make the greatest contribution to tariff making in the nation's history." While the president had gotten some of the flexibility he wanted, it was not as much as he had hoped.

During his second state of the union address, Harding returned to tariffs and the new law: "The enactment has imposed a large responsibility upon the [president and executive branch], but that responsibility will be discharged with a broad mindfulness of the whole business situation."[14] Nonetheless, Harding soon found that the new law was not sufficiently flexible to prevent repercussions, and agriculture was first to suffer from the high tariffs, followed soon by other industries in later years. Had Harding lived he might have given further thought to tariffs. While in office he remained favorable to protective tariffs. So too did his successors (Coolidge and Hoover), until the American financial system collapsed in 1929, with tariffs playing their own role in the financial market's crash.[15]

No presidential action by Harding was more discerning nor longer-lasting than his imposition of business practices on government. As requested by Harding, the special session of the 67th Congress enacted the Budget and Accounting Act of 1921 and Harding signed it on June 10, 1921. The statute placed the Bureau of the Budget in the Treasury Department (next door to the White House). The budget director was made directly responsible to the president and not to the secretary of the Treasury or any other cabinet officer. In addition, the new law established the General Accounting Office to assure congressional oversight of federal expenditures. To launch the new law Harding asked Charlie Dawes to come to Washington. Dawes agreed to do so for one year with one condition—that Harding promise to back him up in his efforts to cut expenditures. Dawes thought he should serve for only a year because his task was going to make him a very

unpopular fellow in Washington. Harding agreed to both conditions and Dawes quickly got busy within the new administration.

Dawes first educated the department and agency heads about the
functions of the new Bureau of the Budget. To do so, Dawes assembled bureau chiefs and higher from the entire executive branch at
the Department of Interior auditorium, with Harding instructing all
to attend. At the first of two sessions, more than twelve hundred
people (including Harding and his entire cabinet) gathered to hear
Dawes's call for thrift, economy, and efficiency. Then a second
group, almost the same size, heard a repeat performance.

Dawes made his point graphically. Carrying two brooms he told
his audience, "This may look like a stage play, but it's not, because
things like this have to stop. Here is a Navy broom, made in accordance with Navy specifications," he announced holding one broom
above his head. "Here is an Army broom made in accordance with
Army specifications," he said holding up the other broom, which
looked identical to the first. "Now, the Army had 350,000 of these
brooms in surplus. The Navy needed 18,000 brooms. It could have
had the Army brooms for nothing but because they were wrapped
with twine instead of wire, the Navy wouldn't take them as a gift.
So the Navy went into the market and bought brooms at top
prices."[16] Such waste of federal money, he said, was to end under
the Harding administration. Harding had asked Dawes to cut $1
billion of federal spending, and with the president's support he did
slightly better. When Dawes left government in 1922, after his one
year, he carried with him as souvenirs his less-than-government-
issue handwritten pasteboard sign from his office door, which read
BUREAU OF THE BUDGET. He had practiced what he preached. His
only extravagance, he also took the two government brooms from
his show-and-tell. Two years later Dawes returned to Washington
to serve as President Calvin Coolidge's vice president.

One of Harding's priorities in his April 12, 1921, message to
Congress was a tax cut. Treasury Secretary Mellon and Commerce

Secretary Hoover believed, and convinced the president, that tax reductions would stimulate the economy. The largest cuts were to be made in the excess profits taxes, but cuts were also to be made in corporate tax rates (then at 10 percent). However, the general income tax rates (then 4 percent on incomes under $4,000 and 8 percent above that amount) were to remain unchanged. In short, it was a tax break for the rich.[17]

Mellon wanted to make up for the lost revenue by taxing bank checks and automobiles and charging more for postcards. The House Ways and Means Committee largely agreed with Mellon's cuts, except for the corporate rate, which they actually increased to 12.5 percent as well as creating a larger exemption for low-income families. When the House bill arrived in the Senate, it was immediately sidetracked by agricultural issues and the soldiers' bonus bill. It emerged only after Harding had his first head-on clash with the Senate, which was determined to adopt a budget-busting, politically popular bonus for World War I veterans. Harding's confrontation with the Senate was one of the defining moments of his presidency, although it is frequently overlooked by Harding's detractors. The Senate's interest in providing a bonus for the soldiers of the world war nearly brought business to a halt, slowing not only the tax legislation but the tariff legislation as well.

Following the war's close in 1918, there had developed a widespread feeling that a bonus of some nature should be granted to the ex-servicemen. By the time the matter reached the front burners in Congress in 1921, thirty-eight states had agreed to grant bonuses, with many of the states amending their constitutions to do so.[18] Washington was under great political pressure to provide an additional bonus, and rising unemployment had exacerbated the situation. The Senate proposed to pay a bonus of $1.25 per day for each day of overseas service during the war ($1.00 for domestic service) with payments to be in quarterly installments, or converted to life insurance at the option of each soldier. Sponsors of the federal bonus were not sure how much it would cost the Treasury, but low estimates were in the billions. Not only would such a bonus preclude Harding from enacting a tax cut; it added to rather than reduced the national debt that had grown excessively during the war, and which Harding was determined to pay down.

On July 6, 1921, and after consultation with Harding, Secretary of the Treasury Mellon sent a letter to the Senate to dissuade senators from acting on the bonus bill. During a lunch the next day with old friends at the Senate, Harding learned that the bonus bill was about to pass. He advised his former colleagues that it was too expensive, and he felt so strongly that he was going to return to the White House to prepare a message on the matter to the Senate. Congressional relations staff did not yet exist in the White House to lobby for a president, so Harding selected the most forceful lobbying technique available—direct intervention by the president.

Six days later, on July 12, Harding returned to the Senate to personally deliver his message and to spend his own political capital to block the bonus bill. Shortly after two o'clock he was escorted to the vice president's desk, where he was introduced and received with a standing ovation before launching directly into the problem. The president explained that "there has come to my attention the pending unfinished business before the Senate, and it is an imperative duty to convey to you the probable effect of the passage at this time of the proposed act providing for adjusted compensation to our service men in the World War." Pulling no punches, he told the Senate that if such action was taken, it would be a "disaster to the Nation's finances" plus it would preclude cutting taxes. Harding gave a surprisingly stern lecture on the nation's finances and the lack of money to pay for such a bonus. He explained what was already being done by a grateful nation for its veterans and it was extensive: compensation and insurance claims numbering 813,442 were pending with half a billion dollars already paid out for such claims; 107,824 men were then enrolled in vocational training or rehabilitation programs for disabled soldiers, which cost $65 million annually; and an estimated additional half billion would be needed before the program ended. When the president said he understood the desire to do something for veterans, no one doubted his sincerity. But they were not pleased to be told they should not "break down our Treasury, from which so much is later on to be expected." The president closed with a request that the Senate get back to work on the matters for which he had called the special session.[19]

Reaction to Harding's personal lobbying was strong. No sooner was the president out of the Senate chamber than progressive Republicans and Democrats went after him for his gumption in coming to the Senate to kill legislation. The partisan debate quickly degenerated. Senators Borah and La Follette were incensed by Harding's action. The remarks of Senator Pat Harrison, a Mississippi Democrat, reflects the attitude of the critics: "It is peculiarly strange, though, it would seem to me, that while in the cases of President Wilson coming to Congress it was in the interest of world peace, world humanity, the enfranchisement of the women of the country, for the ship purchase bill, and other constructive legislation, yet the only time the present President has come before the Senate has been in an obstructive way, and he has attacked the soldiers of America who fought and won the recent war."[20] But the critics were in the minority. The press applauded Harding's going to the Senate, noting his "outstanding courage," "intelligence," and "patriotism." The *New York Times* said Harding had shown himself "President of the whole people, not an opportunist politician," and joined in endorsing the president's request that the Senate put aside the bonus bill.[21] The president's efforts were successful. The Senate followed his advice and sent the bonus bill back to committee. But it was not dead, only resting.

Harding's July 12, 1921, message did nudge the Senate to take action on the tax legislation, although they did not get it resolved until September, when Senator Boies Penrose, who had been diagnosed with terminal cancer, made the tax bill his last great cause. Penrose, who had been Mellon's principal sponsor for the cabinet, was able to guide the House tax bill through the Senate Finance Committee and, while it ran into stiff opposition from farm-bloc senators and Democrats, it passed. The differences with the House version were ironed out before the close of the special session for the president's signature. This completed the priority items Harding had requested that Congress deal with but certainly did not solve all the problems or resolve the bonus bill.

During the next session, in 1922, the House again passed a soldiers' bonus with a decisive vote of 333 to 70. The House bill made no provision for funding the bonus, thus it was a budget-breaker requiring payment from the Treasury. It was, once again, precisely the type of deficit spending Harding and his secretary of the Treasury had earlier opposed. The president informed the Senate that if they passed the bill, he would veto it. Harding's announced veto resulted in heavy lobbying of the White House first by the Senate, and then by the heavy guns of the American Legion. But they could not change Harding's mind. The Senate passed the bonus bill by a vote of 36 to 17, a tally that showed that many senators wanted to avoid being on the record for more deficit spending, and also that they did not want to be on the record opposing the politically popular bonus in an election year.

Conventional wisdom expected Harding to cave and reluctantly sign the bonus measure. On September 19, 1922, he surprised many by vetoing the bill only six weeks before the election. Expressing his sympathy for the plight of veterans, he declared that it was simply unfair to add to the national debt for fewer than 5 million veterans at the expense of 110 million Americans; "whether inspired by grateful sentiment or political expediency," it would undermine the confidence on which the nation's credit was built and "establish the precedent of distributing public funds whenever the proposal and numbers affected make it seem politically appealing to do so."[22] The House overrode the veto. But the Senate sustained it. It was a bold stand by the president in an election year, and it hurt him politically in the short term. He did not live long enough to fully appreciate the significance of his position, which helped to usher in the booming economy of the roaring twenties.

In his April 12, 1921, message to Congress, Harding had expressed his determination to deal with the farmers' plight. Farmers had experienced a rapid decline in agricultural prices following the war. During the campaign Secretary Wallace had suggested that the president call a conference to focus on the crisis. The conference was to educate both the government about the problems and farmers about what government could and could not do. Initially, Secretaries Mellon and Hoover opposed any such conference for fear that industrial leaders might think the administration was favoring agriculture. Animosity between Hoover and Wallace predated their arrival in Harding's cabinet; Wallace had a dim view of Hoover's purchasing of agricultural products in 1918 as Food Administrator.[23] Harding sided with Wallace, who regularly sought out the president for a round of golf, where he could make his pitch. Working with Wallace, and by use of a bipartisan farm bloc of senators and representatives in Congress, Harding made significant progress. Harding was not able to solve the myriad problems that had befallen farmers, but his efforts kept a bad situation from becoming worse.

The agricultural conference was convened on January 23, 1922. Delegates from thirty-seven states were invited and the 336 official delegates represented a diverse group of farm organizations, political leaders, and agricultural economists.[24] Harding opened the conference. He assured farmers that they were not alone in the period of adjustment the nation was going through and that his administration understood their plight and pledged action. "Now, in his hour of disaster, consequent of the reaction from the feverish conditions of war, [the farmer] comes to us asking that he be given support and assistance which shall testify to our appreciation of his service," Harding said describing the situation. "To this he is entitled, not only for the service he has done [during the war], but because if we fail him we will precipitate a disaster that will affect every industrial and commercial activity of the Nation."[25] The president's lengthy address showed both knowledge of agricultural problems and empathy for farmers. His administration had not forgotten farmers.

By the autumn 1922 midterm election, Secretary Wallace was telling farm audiences of significant accomplishments of the administration. For example, he told an audience in Greensburg, Indiana: "Since March 1921 agriculture has had more attention and sympathetic consideration in the national capital than any other like period in our history."[26] And he backed up his assurance with a litany of accomplishments: "capital of the Farm Land Banks was doubled, Joint Land Banks were allowed to modify [and lower] interest rates, the life of the War Finance Corporation had been extended, cooperatives were exempted from anti-trust prosecution by passage of the Capper-Volstead Act [often called agriculture's Magna Carta], an amendment of the Federal Reserve Act allowed the appointment of an agricultural representative, enactment of the Grain Futures Trading Act regulated speculation on the commodity market and passage of the Packers and Stockyard Act insured fair practices on the part of the meat packing industry."[27] It was an impressive listing.

Following the 1922 election more favorable legislation and executive actions were adopted for farmers. The combined efforts of President Harding and his agriculture secretary were significant. They repeatedly went to Congress with farm issues, where they were joined by farm lobby organizations and the power of the farm bloc in Congress. In addition, Harding used his vice president, Calvin Coolidge, as the presiding officer of the Senate, to push the president's legislation through that chamber.[28] So remarkable were Harding's efforts on behalf of farmers that later commentators observed that "[t]he amount of progressive-type legislation during [Harding's brief presidency] was not duplicated again until the days of the New Deal."[29] Harding's efforts brought prosperity to farmers; had his successors Coolidge and Hoover been as aggressive as Harding, the farm problem might have been solved.

Other than his success with farm-related legislation, the emergency tariffs, and creation of the Bureau of the Budget, Harding got little else out of the special session of the 67th Congress, and not much more out of the regular session. Some have suggested that Harding might have gotten more if he had exercised more leadership; this isn't clear.

Lindsay Rogers, Columbia professor of political science (in 1921–22) who later was part of FDR's "brain trust," contemporaneously followed the Harding administration closely. In 1924 he wrote that notwithstanding Harding's initial hands-off approach, "Congress [was] becoming increasingly difficult" to lead, "partly on account of insurgent elements in the Republican party, and partly on account of the procedures in the House and Senate."[30] Rogers notes that this was unlike the situation when Theodore Roosevelt was president and Republicans controlled Congress. At that time Republican Speaker Joe Cannon could deliver the House to the president, and such legislation then proceeded easily through the Republican Senate because filibusters were rare. In short, Professor Rogers is saying that had Harding chosen to more aggressively lead Congress, it is not likely that he would have succeeded.

Professor Rogers noted that Harding was honoring his campaign pledge to stay off the back of Congress, but Rogers surmised, "Mr. Harding probably regretted his promise not to use the lash."[31] Unknown to Rogers and other commentators at the time was the fact that Harding was, in truth, actively reassessing his position. Harding wrote his longtime friend Malcolm Jennings in July 1921, "I find I can not carry out my pre-election ideals of an Executive keeping himself aloof from Congress," adding in a later letter, "One gets a very different view of Congress from the Executive office than I have ever entertained heretofore. Indeed, one gets a very different view of all problems of government. Responsibility has a strange effect. [One is] imbued with the desire to serve above and beyond most selfish aims. I find even myself growing less a partisan than I once was."[32] By early 1923, Harding had become more assertive with Congress, a fact that may explain the institutional inclination of Congress to later aggressively investigate the Harding administration, and send a message to later presidents.

No problem was more serious for the Harding administration than the pervasive labor unrest that he inherited. Following the armistice, the uneasy wartime truce between management and labor had fallen apart. Harding found his administration facing growing discontent in the labor movement, with communist organizers and agitators seeking to take advantage of the disquiet. In his inaugural address, the president had appealed to both sides: "My most reverent prayer for America is for industrial peace," and he called for both sides to settle their disputes at "the conference table in advance," rather than after the breakdown of communications. He hoped for "an era of good feeling," but it was not to be. Harding was confronted by two of the most serious strikes of the decade in 1922. Union strength had grown during the world war and management wanted to dilute that power once the war ended. Management sought to break union power by reducing employee wages, using the faltering economy as an excuse.

Harding's views of labor, formed during his days at the *Marion Star*, "were essentially conservative and paternalistic," according to his biographer Randolph Downes, who says that Harding felt that management knew what was best for labor and that "[s]trikes which interfered with the right to work were wrong." Downes adds that Harding especially had no tolerance for "[u]nions . . . led by demagogues who relied on threats and violence."[33] Harding's personal experience with labor was somewhat of an anomaly. Notwithstanding Marion's sizable manufacturing operations, all were open shops; it was a nonunion town. Yet the *Marion Star* was unionized. In fact, Harding had encouraged the union, and even provided office space for the Marion Typographical Union. Thus, he was anything but antilabor.[34]

Harding's most pro-labor act as president was to employ the persuasive powers of his office, and his philosophy of conciliation, to end the steel industry's twelve-hour workday (although it did not happen until the day he died).[35] Before the strikes, he also called a nonpartisan unemployment conference in Washington on September 26, 1921, where he acknowledged to the three hundred delegates that "there is excessive unemployment today and we are concerned, not alone about its diminution, but we are frankly anxious, under the involved conditions, lest it grow worse, with hardships of the winter season soon to be met."[36] The conference produced a host of recommendations, several of which Harding immediately implemented. Probably the most helpful was his prodding state and local governments to commence public works projects that would provide employment. The president took similar action at the federal level, ordering all his cabinet secretaries to look for federal projects that could be started sooner rather than later. Harding's pump priming, which was contrary to his philosophy of using federal funds to solve the unemployment problem, certainly helped. Harding is credited with halting the increase of unemployment that confronted his administration and keeping suffering at a minimum; in fact, he actually obtained a slight decline in unemployment figures.[37] By calling for conciliation in 1921 Harding also averted a nationwide rail strike.

The labor situation worsened the next year, however. By April 1922, 400,000 bituminous-coal miners went on strike to preserve the gains they had made during the war years. Given the strenuous nature of their labor, they were also demanding a five-day workweek at six hours per day. On the other side of the issue, the bituminous-coal operators wanted to reduce wages of their miners to bring down the production cost of coal; they insisted on maintaining the existing eight-hour day and a six-day week.[38] Harding believed the proper role for the president was to monitor the situation, remain uncommitted, and work behind the scenes to resolve the dispute—which he did.

The circumstances became dire when railroad shop workers also struck for very similar reasons. While the railway shop workers' situation was a bit more complex, involving the Railroad Labor Board, it came down to a wage cut and working hours as well. Both coal operators and railroads continued operating with strike breakers replacing those on the picket lines, which provoked eruptions of violence around the nation.

To resolve the coal strike, Harding invited the heads of the coal unions and operators to the White House, including John L. Lewis, the best known of the labor leaders. Using the threat of government intervention, the president asked the two sides to negotiate a settlement in good faith. He charged Secretaries Hoover, Davis, and Fall with supervising the negotiations. By mid-July, it was evident that no acceptable solution would be found. Rather than fail, Harding laid before the two sides a plan to resume work under existing pay and time schedules until a commission he would appoint could investigate and make recommendations fair to all.[39] Harding's move was reminiscent of Theodore Roosevelt's coal strike plan in 1902.[40] But it didn't work for Harding. Although the plan was accepted by several coal operators, it was rejected by John L. Lewis's United Mine Workers. Harding decided he could do no more, so he asked the mine operators to resume production to assure that the nation had ample fuel for the winter, operating as best they could. Harding made his disappointment obvious in a statement he released at the White House: "I have heard your decision. I would not be frank if I did not confess a disappointment in your lack of unanimity. To the large majority, who have pledged readiness to resume activities under the government proposal, I must express my own and the public's gratitude. We have reached a point, owing to the refusal of mine-workers and a minority of your operators to accept the proposed arbitration, where the good offices of the government . . . are without avail."[41] Harding sent a telegram to the governors of the states with mining operations advising them of the situation, and assuring them "of the prompt and full support of the federal government" should it be necessary to maintain law and order.[42]

Harding acted without favoring either side, but neither side viewed it that way. "[Harding was] pilloried on the one hand by operators for not *forcing* the striking miners to return, and on the other by the United Mine Workers for extending protection to any who did [resume operation.]"[43] He found himself in a similar no-win situation with the railroad shop workers strike, whose strikes were plagued with increasing violence.[44] In an effort to resolve the rail dispute, Harding developed a proposed resolution working with Secretaries Davis and Hoover, and in consultation with a member of the Railroad Labor Board, which was submitted to the parties on July 31, 1922. It was rejected, however, by railroad executives (specifically because of the provision permitting striking employees to return with no loss of position or seniority) but was accepted in full by the unions. When Harding suggested submitting the matter of seniority to the Labor Board for resolution after workers returned, the unions rejected the counteroffer but the rail executives accepted it. It was an impossible situation.

The cabinet was divided on how to resolve the strikes, and the dangers they posed to economic recovery. Attorney General Harry Daugherty, who was antiunion, was the most aggressive, seeking Harding's approval to find a way to arrest all the strikers. Daugherty believed it was the work of the communists. The president, however, did not see it that way. Because there was no easy solution, Harding felt it necessary to advise the Congress, and the public, regarding the impasse. On August 18, 1922, at a joint session of the House and Senate, the president summarized the situation. "I should be remiss if I failed frankly to lay the matter before you and at the same time acquaint you and the whole people with such efforts as the executive branch of Government has made," he began. After setting forth the facts regarding the coal strike, he reported, "The Government being without authority to enforce a strike settlement in the coal industry," he could only volunteer his good offices "in finding a way of adjustment." He walked Congress through his efforts and told them of the underlying problem: that there were more bituminous-coal mines operating, and more mine workers seeking jobs, than necessary to supply the country. Harding felt at "the moment the coal skies are clearing," but he was looking for a permanent solution to avoid the problem recurring every year. "I have an unalterable conviction that no lasting satisfactory or worth-while results will ensue unless we may have a Government commission, independent of the industry, clothed with authority by Congress to search deeply, so that it may advise as to fair wages and as to conditions of labor, and recommend the enactment of laws to protect the public in the further." Harding's suggestion was actually pro-labor in seeking this essential information because operators had refused to provide it to the government. In addition, he asked Congress to create an emergency agency to acquire coal and stockpile it, so profit seekers could not take advantage of the current situation and price-gouge consumers in the coming winter.

The president's address turned to the railway shop workers strike. Again he reported his unsuccessful efforts to mediate the differences. He spared neither side as he laid out the failed negotiations. At "the present moment," he said, "the developments which have heightened the Government's concern" were the violence and the fact that other unions were threatening to strike in sympathy. But more troublesome was the fact that those sympathizing with rail workers were beginning to disrupt interstate commerce. Continental trains were abandoned in the southwestern deserts, and the violence was escalating beyond mere scuffles. Those who had refused to strike "have been cruelly attacked and wounded or killed." It was a federal problem because local and state governments were refusing to provide protection to those crossing picket lines, and other industries were now being hurt by the transportation breakdowns, particularly fruit growers and farmers. Harding sought no congressional action on the rail strike, however. "No hasty action would contribute to the solution of the present critical situation," he said. And with one exception, there were ample federal laws, civil and criminal, to deal with offenders. The exception was the "pitiable sense of Federal impotence to deal with the shocking crime at Herrin, Ill., which so recently shamed and horrified the country." He was referring to an incident where nineteen strikebreakers and two strikers had been killed by union men and the state and local authorities refused to prosecute the murderers. The federal government was without legal author- ity to do so, and he wanted a law to fill this gap so that all Ameri- cans would be safe.[45]

Congress appreciated Harding's approach. The only criticism from Capitol Hill was that he should have enlisted their assistance sooner. Both labor and management were critical of Harding's speech and his approach. With neither side liking Harding's posi- tion, the usually anti-Harding *New Republic* decided the president must be right and proclaimed his approach to the problem better than either labor or management.[46]

Additional efforts by the president to get the rail strike re- solved failed. In conversations with Secretary Hoover and Senator Albert Cummins, Harding considered taking over the railroads and ordering the strikers back to work. He abandoned this idea when it became clear that the House of Representatives would kill any such action.[47]

The strikes, which were consuming the president and his cabi- net, appear to have been resolved during a long weekend outing of which no record was made, and which none of those involved ever reported. But the sequence of events speaks for itself.

On Saturday, August 26, 1922, the presidential yacht, the

Mayflower, departed Washington for a three-day cruise. Accompanying the president were Senators Kellogg, Cummins, and Watson, along with Representative Winslow in the congressional contingency; and from his cabinet were Secretaries Hoover and Fall, along with Attorney General Daugherty; and lastly the man Harding had convinced to return to Washington to run the Shipping Board, Albert Lasker. All these men had been involved with the strikes, either officially or unofficially. Precisely what happened during this voyage, and any deliberations, remains a mystery. It is what happened immediately after the cruise that suggests that these men, notwithstanding later denials, decided on drastic action to resolve the rail strike. As soon as the *Mayflower* returned to Washington on August 29, Daugherty went to his office, and then virtually disappeared, his office reporting that he had gone to Columbus, Ohio, on personal business. In fact, he was en route to Chicago and the U.S. District Court to enjoin the strikers and their leaders.

Historian Colin J. Davis has pieced together the facts from archival records of the Department of Justice. It appears that when Daugherty returned to his office on August 29 from the weekend outing on the *Mayflower,* he was hell-bent on getting an injunction. Working with Justice Department lawyers, he began preparing his case and making arrangements to bring it before a Chicago judge who had jurisdiction over the union and its leaders in Illinois. Professor Davis reports:

> During the last week in August, Justice Department lawyers put together a bill in equity for a federal injunction against the strike. Hubert Work, the postmaster general, had provided the Justice Department with figures on mail trains either canceled or interfered with. Daugherty also readied federal judge James H. Wilkerson, whom he had appointed to the United States District Court of Illinois on July 23. Judge Wilkerson had already involved himself in the strike

by issuing an injunction against the strikers on the Elgin and Joliet Railroad. . . . Appearing before Wilkerson on September 1, Daugherty presented the government's case asking for a restraining order. Citing incidences of violence and the interruption of U.S. mail service and interstate commerce, Daugherty called for an order that would prevent the encouragement of the strike by the strikers' leadership. Not surprisingly, Wilkerson . . . handed down one of the most sweeping federal injunctions in U.S. history.[48]

The Wilkerson injunction effectively ended the strike. It also stunned several members of Harding's cabinet, who were not privy to Daugherty's plans. The *New York Times* found it "a startling surprise." Labor leaders were apoplectic over the president's bold move, which Harding, in a letter to Charles Dawes, explained, "We are going to have a great deal of grief uttered by Mr. Gompers and his shouting associates, but the government is really doing nothing to enslave workmen . . . [it] is trying to maintain a state of freedom and security in which men may work as they choose to do." Harding added that the move had been anything but hasty: "The court action taken last week was pretty drastic but it was well considered and very much deliberated on before the [action] was finally taken."[49] While the Wilkerson injunction solved the problem, it earned Harding the everlasting resentment of labor, unfairly labeling him an antilabor president. It earned Daugherty a bill of impeachment in the House of Representatives, which he survived, but not without a lot of bad press. The American people, however, were mostly grateful for Harding's firm handling of the strike.

No decision that a president makes is likely to have a more lasting impact than his selecting a member of the U.S. Supreme Court. Before Harding's presidency ended he made four Supreme Court selections. When Chief Justice Edward White died on May 19,

1921, rumors were circulating that Associate Justice John H. Clarke, who had been appointed by Woodrow Wilson, was also about to retire. Harding had told former president Taft that he would nominate him for the Court. Taft was interested only in being chief justice.[50] Harding briefly delayed sending Taft's name to the Senate because he also hoped to nominate his friend and political adviser former senator George Sutherland, to whom Harding had also promised a seat on the Court. When it became clear that Justice Clarke was not about to resign (he would do so a year later and Sutherland would be nominated at that time), Harding nominated Taft as chief justice, and he was quickly confirmed.

Like many presidents, Harding maintained an informal working relationship with Chief Justice Taft regarding the Court's vacancies. In addition to appointing Taft (1921) and Sutherland (1922), both being purely Harding's selections, he appointed two additional justices: Pierce Butler (1923) and Edward T. Sanford (1923). These latter appointees Harding selected based on Taft's recommendation. U.S. Supreme Court historian Henry J. Abraham reports that Supreme Court experts rank Taft (who served until 1930) as a "near great" chief justice; and Sutherland (who served until 1938) was also considered a "near great" associate justice. As for Butler (who served until 1939), the legal historians rank him as a "failure." Harding's last appointee, Sanford (who served until 1930), has not been ranked by Professor Abraham, although he does note that Sanford's landmark opinion in *Gitlow* v. *New York* established "that freedom of speech and of the press . . . are among the fundamental personal rights and 'liberties' protected by the due process of law clause of the Fourteenth Amendment from impairment by the States [as well as by the federal government]."

By any historical criteria, Harding's selections to the U.S. Supreme Court were quite strong. Harding knew the men he was placing on the Court, particularly with Taft and Sutherland. At the time Harding selected Taft, the Supreme Court still sat in the

Capitol Building, using the old Senate chamber as its courtroom with its staff and offices scattered about the building. Taft saw to it that the high Court would become a fully coequal branch of government as far as facilities, and the present Supreme Court building stands as a monument to his undertaking. As chief justice, Taft sought, and largely succeeded, to make the Supreme Court a model of court efficiency. As a legal scholar, Taft led an activist majority that construed government power narrowly. But Harding's sending Taft, and his other selections, to the Supreme Court did not win him any friends in the African-American community. The Taft Court did little for civil rights, and blacks had hoped for better from Harding.

During the 1920 campaign, on two occasions, and then following his election, Harding had met with James Weldon Johnson of the National Association for the Advancement of Colored People (NAACP), thus giving black voters hope that the new president might address their grievances. Johnson, who had been one of five blacks on a GOP advisory committee for the platform, was a noted songwriter, poet, and author (pseudonymously of *The Autobiography of an Ex-Colored Man*). He and Harding had a good rapport, and they met for a fourth time on April 4, 1921, shortly after Harding assumed office. At this meeting Johnson spoke "frankly of the great unrest among colored people and their dissatisfaction with the conditions which allowed lynching, disfranchisement, peonage [a situation where a debtor is forced to work for a creditor until a debt was paid] and other forms of racial injustice."[51]

After his meeting with Johnson, Harding not only made additions to his special message to Congress; he also spoke with Attorney General Daugherty. This is evident from Daugherty's April 9 letter to the NAACP acknowledging that peonage "exist[ed] to a shocking extent in Georgia, Alabama, and some parts of Texas," and that the Justice Department was prosecuting all such cases. Black hopes were "aroused" by the call to end lynching in Harding's April 12 special message to Congress, and the House's passage of the antilynching legislation. Understandably, blacks were disappointed when the legislation was stopped in the Senate by filibustering Southern Democrats. Nor could blacks find much hope in the efforts of Harding's Justice Department to deal with disfranchisement, for the efforts were nominal in assuring blacks their right to vote.

James Johnson had urged Harding to appoint blacks to the posts in government they had held *before* Wilson's administration. Notwithstanding his progressive thinking on most matters, Wilson had excluded and segregated blacks as he had remained rooted in his Southern ways. As one commentator wrote, Wilson's policies worsened the situation for Harding because "the bitterness engendered by Democratic policies encouraged [blacks] to look once more to the GOP."[52] Harding did appoint blacks to high-level posts in the Departments of Labor and Interior, plus the president's staff sent memoranda to all the cabinet, seeking positions for qualified blacks. Harding appointed a black as minister to Liberia and found three more important posts from his survey of the cabinet.[53]

Within the first six months in office, Harding placed an additional 140 blacks in lesser posts, and some 24 percent of the District of Columbia post office employees were black. But this was really just tokenism. In fairness to Harding, however, he was greatly restricted in obtaining the pre-Wilson level of appointments because Wilson had removed Republicans and blacks from appointed positions, replaced them with white Democrats, and then locked them into the system by extending civil service protections. In short, Harding did not have the spoils that Wilson had taken out of play. Harding was frustrated that he could not do more, but as he privately conceded to his friend Malcolm Jennings in a letter that today might be misconstrued as even racist, he felt, rightly or wrongly, that he could never do enough: "The Negroes are very hard to please. If they could have half of the Cabinet, seventy-five per cent of the Bureau Chiefs, two-thirds of the Diplomatic appointments and all of the officers to enforce prohibition perhaps there would be a measure of contentment temporarily, but I do not think it would long abide."[54]

Great numbers of blacks still found Harding's heart and head in the right place and, giving him the benefit of their doubts, felt his failures could "be explained partly in terms of his lack of awareness of the urgency behind the demands of an increasing number of Negro leaders" and that "the NAACP intended its program to be one for immediate action, not merely long-range planning."[55] Clearly, Harding was thinking long term. In fact, he hoped to reshape the Republican Party during his presidency by bringing the South, including blacks, back within the party. It was a delicate move by Harding to even consider creating a two-party South, and difficult to accomplish without offending sensitivities, either white or black. To launch this initiative he traveled on October 26, 1921, to Woodrow Wilson Park in Birmingham, Alabama, to speak about civil rights before a large, albeit segregated, audience of blacks and whites. To say it was a bold and atypical in-your-face move by Harding toward Democratic officeholders in the South is an understatement. It was no doubt the most daring and controversial speech of Harding's political career.

Harding unflinchingly told his Southern audience, and the rest of the world, that it was time for political and economic equality of the races. "When I suggest the possibility of economic equality between the races, I mean it precisely the same way and to the same extent that I would mean it if I spoke of equality of economic opportunity as between members of the same race. In each case I would mean equality proportional to the honest capacities and deserts of the individual." Harding made clear as well what he meant by political equality. "I would say let the black man vote when he is fit to vote; prohibit the white man voting when he is unfit to vote." His stunned white audience sat in stony silence, reported the *New York News,* as Harding "squared his jaw and pointed straight at the white section" and declared, "Whether you like it or not, unless our democracy is a lie you must stand for that equality."[56]

Then the president turned to education. "I would insist upon equal educational opportunity," he announced. Harding conceded that he did not foresee an easy dissolution of barriers between the races, nor did he have an answer for creating "social equality." But he knew how the process must start. He said, "There must be such education among the colored people as will enable them to develop their own leaders, capable of understanding and sympathizing with such differentiation between the races as I have suggested. . . . Racial amalgamation there cannot be. Partnership of the races in developing the highest aims of all humanity there must be if humanity, not only here but everywhere, is to achieve the ends which we have set for it."[57] Harding's Birmingham speech received mixed reactions. Not surprisingly, it outraged most Southerners. And some blacks took offense to Harding's bluntness about the difficulty of social equality, while others believed he was only being candid. Dr. Robert R. Moton of the Tuskegee Institute called the speech the "most important utterance on the question by a President since Lincoln"; W. E. B. Du Bois praised all but the comments on social equality; and even the outspoken black "back to Africa" organizer Marcus Garvey offered praise.

Harding's presidency ended before his actions could equal his words, leaving the hopes of African-Americans unfulfilled.

To those critics who believed they had correctly pigeonholed Harding, his treatment of the imprisoned Socialist leader Eugene Debs was more of a shock than his Birmingham speech. Harding began thinking about Debs long before entering the White House, as early as his days in the Senate. A reporter from the Cleveland *Plain Dealer*, Clyde R. Miller, who had testified against Debs at his trial in 1918, had visited Harding in the Senate. Debs had been convicted of sedition for speaking against the war effort. Miller had had second thoughts about Debs and his testimony and wanted Senator Harding to use any influence he might have to get Debs freed. There was nothing, however, that Senator Harding could do, for President Wilson, who had prosecuted Debs, wanted Debs in prison. Even as the Wilson administration was coming to an end, when Wilson's attorney general, A. Mitchell Palmer, sent a recommendation to Wilson to pardon Debs, the largely incapacitated Wilson personally wrote on the petition—"Denied."[58] Shortly before his inauguration Harding told Harry Daugherty, his soon-to-be attorney general, that he wanted to commute Debs's sentence as well as the sentences of others convicted of sedition during the war.

Debs, who was sixty-five years of age and in good health, had been given a ten-year sentence, which he was serving in the federal penitentiary in Atlanta. After conferring with Harding, Daugherty sent for Debs to come to Washington to visit him. At Harding's direction, Debs traveled to and from Washington by himself without a guard. The attorney general, who initially had misgivings about releasing Debs, was impressed. Daugherty later reported, "We talked freely for several hours. He unfolded frankly his ideas on government, his ideas on religion, his own case, the cause of Socialism . . . his beliefs and disbeliefs. A more eloquent and fascinating recital I never heard fall from the lips of any man. . . . I found him a charming personality, with a deep love for his fellow man—to my mind, of course, absolutely wrong in his ideas on government and society, yet always sincere, truthful and honest."[59]

Opposition arose as soon as it became known that Harding was considering the release of Debs, with none more adamant than the politically powerful American Legion and none closer to home than Florence Harding. Even the *New York Times* urged Harding not to free Debs; "He is where he belongs. He should stay there." And the *Times* warned that "the majority of the American people will not approve of this commutation."[60] Those encouraging Harding to free Debs were certainly not men and women who had voted Harding into office, people like George Bernard Shaw, H. G. Wells, Clarence

Darrow, and Upton Sinclair.[61] Newsman and editor William Allen
White accompanied a group of Debs supporters to the White
House, where a woman in the group interrupted President Harding
as he was explaining his thinking: "Mr. President, that's no way to
answer us," she announced. "We demand a yes-or-no answer now!"
William Allen White, no fan of Harding's (as he later made clear),
recorded the event: "We were shocked. . . . But the President
straightened himself up. The stoop seemed to come out of his
shoulders. A certain dignity enveloped him. He said: 'My dear
woman, you may demand anything you please out of Warren Harding. He will not resent it. But the President of the United States
has the right to keep his own counsel, and the office I occupy for-
bids me to reply to you as I should like to do if I were elsewhere!'"[62]

Harding, in fact, had already made up his mind. But he felt that
he must wait until the nation was not technically still at war.
Accordingly, as soon as Germany ratified the peace treaty with the
United States in November 1921, Harding instructed Daugherty
to prepare the clemency papers for Debs. Daugherty suggested
year-end, but Harding insisted by Christmas, with a request that
Debs drop by the White House on his way home to Indiana.
When Debs walked out of his Atlanta cell on December 23, 1921,
every one of the twenty-three hundred federal prisoners cheered
him. This did not surprise the warden, who had told Daugherty
that Debs "had been like a breath of fresh air to the men with
whom he came in contact," and he "was a great help in the main-
tenance of discipline."[63]

Little is known of the meeting between Harding and Debs at
the White House. When Debs was ushered into the Oval Office,
Harding bounded out of his chair to greet him. "Well, I've heard so
damned much about you, Mr. Debs, that I am now glad to meet
you personally." After a lengthy private conversation, Debs
departed, and he was swarmed by reporters. What did he think of
Harding? "Mr. Harding appears to me to be a kind gentleman, one

whom I believe possesses humane impulses," was all he chose to ever say, and then he headed home to Indiana.

In responding privately to his friend Malcolm Jennings, who couldn't understand why Harding had released Debs, the president replied, "I was persuaded in my own mind that it was the right thing to do. . . . I thought the spirit of clemency was quite in harmony with the things we were trying to do here in Washington."[64] Harding was trying to return the nation to a lasting peace, to "normalcy." Debs and others imprisoned because of the war were lingering remnants of events he wanted behind the nation. Rather than grant general amnesty, Harding reviewed each case, and so long as no violent or destructive acts had occurred, he proceeded to free those jailed under the Sedition Act, a law that had been repealed. At the time he freed Debs, he was taking actions he hoped might formalize the spirit of harmony he mentioned to Jennings, an effort to do no less than eliminate the prospect of another war any time soon by disarming the major powers of the world, and resolving remaining potential territorial conflicts in the Pacific. To do this Harding called an historic disarmament conference in the nation's capital.

Warren Harding had seen more of the world than most of his presidential predecessors, and he had learned much of the workings of American foreign policy during his service on the Senate Foreign Relations Committee. He had once wanted to serve as ambassador to Japan. Yet as president he had no interest in being his own secretary of state. Rather, he developed a highly compatible working relationship with his secretary of state, Charles Evans Hughes.

The rather austere Secretary Hughes found he worked well with the genial and politically savvy Harding. Both men benefited from the relationship, as did the nation. "It is remarkable how well Hughes and Harding were able to work together, for their backgrounds and personalities differed markedly," writes Nan Jamieson Lowerre in her dissertation study of Harding's foreign policy. Dr.

Lowerre explains the association: "Harding expected the State Department to provide him with a concise summary of any problem which arose, along with a suggested solution which the President could either approve or disapprove." Dr. Lowerre believes that "Harding's decision to make Hughes his Secretary of State and to rely almost entirely on his judgment was the most significant foreign policy decision he made as President."[65] There is no question that in selecting Hughes to run the State Department Harding had given the responsibility to a man of enormous ability. Yet Harding remained involved in foreign policy and his role cannot be overlooked so easily.

Harding and Hughes first worked together to end the nation's technical state of war with Germany, Austria, and Hungary, which was a delicate situation given the bloc of senators who believed that any foreign agreements (even to make peace) were bad. Then the president and his secretary of state turned to the demand of Senator William Borah, the often boorish Idaho Republican, who was insisting that the president call a conference with Great Britain and Japan to reduce the construction of naval ships. Costly international naval rivalries had been hotly debated during the final weeks of the prior Congress, and Borah had succeeded in getting the Senate to pass a resolution calling for such an international conference. Harding believed that the Senate had no business trying to run the nation's foreign policy, an executive branch function, although he was not opposed to such a conference. So the president told his former colleagues he would consider a conference, but only on his terms.

After informal diplomatic inquiries revealed that all the relevant parties were receptive to a Washington conference on the limitation of armament, it was announced and invitations were sent out. The conference was planned down to the last detail, for Harding knew the world would be watching. He had been highly critical of Woodrow Wilson's personal involvement in the day-to-day negotiations of the Treaty of Versailles and League of Nations, during which time Wilson had abdicated many of his other presidential responsibilities. Accordingly, Harding and Hughes agreed how best to employ their respective strengths. It was agreed that Harding would remain behind the scenes, except to set the tone and mood for the conference, and he would use his high office to maintain a spirit of goodwill by privately entertaining the visiting diplomats at an array of White House lunches and state dinners.[66] They also decided the United States would boldly take the initiative calling for a drastic reduction of arms, a secret that was closely guarded for a maximum dramatic impact at the opening of the conference.

By early November 1921, invited foreign dignitaries began arriving in Washington from Japan, China, Italy, France, Great Britain, Belgium, the Netherlands, and Portugal. Most of the foreign guests attended the Armistice Day ceremonies held at the new amphitheater at the Arlington National Cemetery on November 11, 1921. President Harding used the occasion of the entombment of America's unknown soldier to speak publicly of the horrors of war. Somberly, solemnly, he talked of the unknown soldier, whose identity "took flight with his imperishable soul. We know not whence he came, but only that his death marks him with the everlasting glory of an American dying for his country." He then talked of the consequences of arms: "It was my fortune recently to see a demonstration of modern warfare. It is no longer a conflict in chivalry, no more a test of militant manhood. It is only cruel, deliberate, scientific destruction." In describing the "rain of ruin from the aircraft" and "the thunder of artillery" and "mortars belching their bombs of desolation" resulting in a "panorama of unutterable destruction," it was not necessary to mention a need for disarmament. Before asking all to join him in the Lord's Prayer, Harding said, "I can sense the prayers of our people, of all peoples, that this Armistice Day shall mark the beginning of a new and lasting era of peace on earth, good will among men."[67] Thousands who heard the president by radio were deeply moved.

Saturday morning, November 12, 1921, Harding formally opened the first plenary session of the conference and used the occasion to speak once again of the evils of war. But this time he did so in the context of "a world staggering with debt" from war, declaring it was a burden that needed to be lifted. "I can speak officially only for our United States. Our hundred million frankly want less of armament and none of war. Wholly free from guile, sure in our own minds that we harbor no unworthy designs, we accredit the world with the same good intent. So I welcome you, not alone in good will and high purpose, but with high faith."[68] With these words, Harding turned the proceedings over to his secretary of state, who headed the American delegation, which Harding and Hughes had carefully selected: Senators Henry Cabot Lodge and Oscar Underwood, a Democrat from Alabama, plus former secretary of state Elihu Root. By preagreement all delegations were small to keep the debate to the minimum.

At the podium, Secretary Hughes first explained why the agenda included questions relating to the Pacific and Far East. It was "not for the purpose of embarrassing or delaying an agreement for arms limitation," rather to take advantage of the opportunity to resolve the problems and controversies. Then Hughes turned to disarmament and moved quickly to his unexpected proposal, which brought gasps from the audience and breathless silence from other delegates:

It would seem to be a vital part of a plan for the limitation of naval armament that there should be a naval holiday. It is proposed that for a period of not less than ten years there should be no further construction of capital ships. I am happy to say that I am at liberty to go beyond these general propositions, and on behalf of the American delegation, acting under instructions of the President of the United States, to submit to you a concrete proposition for an agreement for the limitation of naval armament.

To prepare for the conference, Hughes and Harding had been at work on that "concrete proposition" for months. Harding was serious about disarmament. And Hughes educated himself about the American naval fleet. With Harding's blessings, Hughes had been banging heads at the Navy Department, which was resistant to cutting its fleet. Harding's move toward disarmament reversed the direction of Wilson, who had ordered construction of additional capital ships just before departing from office. Both Harding and Hughes knew that if the United States did not cut back, they could not expect Great Britain or Japan to sign on. If there was no change in direction, there would continue a costly if not deadly contest to see who could build the most warships. Hughes's stunning initiative gave the United States an advantage, and he quickly seized the moment. Hughes informed the delegates that the United States was calling for a tonnage ratio for American-British-Japanese warships of 5–5–3, with Japan at the low ratio. To meet the proposed goal the United States had to scrap ships amounting to 845,000 tons, Great Britain needed to scrap 583,000 tons, and Japan 480,000 tons.

The conference produced monumental results relatively quickly. By early February 1922, the participants had agreed upon eight treaties or understandings, limiting arms (including poison gas) and resolving disputed territorial possessions in the Pacific. There was also a working resolution of tariff issues. Dr. Lowerre says that the conference provided "solutions to many of the pressing foreign policy problems which faced President Harding and Secretary Hughes when they took office. . . . First, the Conference brought an end to an expensive and largely futile race in battleship construction. Second, it provided for the continuation (some thought the strengthening) of the traditional 'open door' policy in China. Third, it solved the ticklish problem of the Anglo-Japanese alliance" that had emerged from World War I. And "[f]inally, the Conference appeared to fulfill Harding's campaign promise of international cooperation without sacrifice of American interests," or, stated more directly, without the League of Nations.[69]

Harding was both pleased and proud of the conference. The State Department legal adviser found that Harding's speech at the close of the conference on February 6, 1922, placed "a mass emotional experience into words . . . so admirably and adequately that no further comment is necessary."[70] Harding simply gave the participants his sincere congratulations and the praise they deserved: "My own gratification is beyond my capacity to express," he said. "This conference has wrought a truly great achievement. It is hazardous sometimes to speak in superlatives, and I will be restrained. But I will say, with every confidence, that the faith plighted here today, kept in national honor, will mark the beginning of a new and better epoch of human progress."

Harding was widely praised for the accomplishments at the Washington disarmament conference. History often passes over Harding's role, claiming it was all the work of Charles Evans Hughes. But, in fact, Harding was deeply involved in the conference, and like so many things he did, his ego did not require that he receive the credit. In fact, there is much evidence of Harding's "hidden hand" not only with the disarmament conference, but with other accomplishments of his presidency.[71] In truth, Harding did what Secretary Hughes could not likely have accomplished without him—made the treaties the law of the land by obtaining Senate approval, which was the make-or-break endgame of the conference.

In a January 1922 visit with H. H. Kohlsaat, publisher of the *Chicago Times-Herald*, Harding shared his thoughts before the fireplace of the Oval Office. "The success or failure of this administration depends on the ratification or rejection of these treaties," Harding said. "Every administration's name in history rests on one or two acts. If these treaties are ratified by the Senate, then this administration's name is secure in history. If these are defeated, nothing I can do the balance of my term can be of more than passing interest, which will be forgotten in a few years."[72]

Even the participation of Senators Lodge and Underwood did not assure easy Senate approval of the treaties produced by the conference. As the simple matter of technically ending hostilities with Germany, Austria, and Hungary had shown, the bloc of "irreconcilable" senators (principally Republicans joined by a few Democrats) was sure to make life difficult for any president, for the irreconcilables were distrustful of such international agreements. Harding employed his considerable political skills in guiding the treaties through the Senate. It was a feat that the politically insensitive Secretary Hughes, who like Wilson earlier had a low tolerance for the pompous Senate, might never have accomplished without Harding. And even then, the president had to accept Senate reservations to some of the provisions. But Harding and Hughes managed to get almost everything they wanted and all that they needed.

In early September 1922, after Harding had put the disarmament conference behind him but was still deeply involved in the coal and rail strikes, a new crisis confronted him. First Lady Florence Harding's bad kidney failed. According to Carl Anthony, the first lady looked death in the eye.[73] Based on reports from her doctors, the president had every reason to believe she was going to die. Dr. Sawyer was joined by the famed Dr. Charles Mayo of Rochester, Minnesota, and a surgeon from nearby Johns Hopkins to deal with Florence Harding's critical condition. Breaking with tradition, the president insisted the public be told of the first lady's grim condition, which resulted in a spontaneous public vigil for the first lady, accompanied by an outpouring of editorials, letters, and flowers sent to the White House. The often abrasive and always assertive woman had won the hearts of Americans, not to mention people throughout the world.

President Harding worked in a study in the White House residence near his wife's sickroom, which he constantly visited. He passed many sleepless nights sitting by his wife's bed gently repeating words she loved from the 121st Psalm, as her temperature climbed to 105 degrees. Her pain was excruciating, notwithstanding regular shots of first codeine, and then opium, which were administered by the nurses in full-time attendance. So severe did the pain become that while semiconscious, the first lady tightened her fist so hard that her fingernails punctured her palms, causing them to bleed. Adding to the president's stress throughout this ordeal was the conflict between the first lady's doctors. The outside experts wanted to operate but homeopathic-trained Dr. Sawyer adamantly refused. He believed her system, with its one floating kidney, would resume working before she died of uremic poisoning. As it happened, he was correct.

On September 13, the newspapers were told the crisis had passed and soon Dr. Mayo went home. Later, Florence Harding described her near-death experience. She had seen her father Amos and other dead relatives, and walked through the "valley of death," as she described it. "There is one thing that counts when you are down in the Valley," she had decided, and that was: "What have you done for human beings? . . . How much have you done for . . . those you love?" It was at that point that she decided to fight for her life, telling herself over and over, "I must not die, Warren needs me," and clenching her fists with determination. Rather than succumb to the pain or the opiates, she walked out of the valley of death.

During the early days of her convalescence the president remained with her, reading to her, or discussing a trip they might take to the West Coast and Alaska. Within a few days she insisted he get back to matters of state full-time, which he did on September 19, 1922, when he vetoed the veterans bonus bill.

8

Death and Disgrace

On December 8, 1922, Harding delivered his second (and last) state of the union message. By this time the economy had recovered and his attention had turned to sustaining economic growth. He offered specific recommendations for internal improvements in reclamation, irrigation, and conservation projects through joint state and federal partnerships and cooperation. He urged faster development of water power and electrical plants. And the pro-business president again showed his progressive streak, when he called for the end of child labor, by constitutional amendment if necessary.[1] His message, and the indications of where he would focus his attention during the remainder of his first term, pleased Congress, the *New York Times*, and even such progressive journals as the *Literary Digest*.[2]

Harding appeared well, and fully in command of his office. Few knew how the stress and strain of his job was seriously taxing an already damaged heart. Being president was not easy for him, notwithstanding his easygoing demeanor. He was a natural at being head of state, but not at the administrative side of the presidency, that of being the head of government. Running the *Marion Star* and a Senate office had provided no transferable experience for running the executive branch of the federal government. After a year at the job Harding admitted, "I never find myself done. I never find myself with my work complete. I don't believe there is a human being who can do all the work there is to be done in the President's office. It seems as though I have been President for twenty years."[3] Without natural executive instincts, he felt himself accountable for virtually every function of his high office, from speechwriting to correspondence. For example, Secretary of State Hughes observed with surprise that Harding dealt personally with vast amounts of White House correspondence and was seldom satisfied with perfunctory responses. And Harding's friend Columbia University president Nicholas Murray Butler once chided the president for personally poring over a stack of letters on his desk, telling him it was ridiculous for him to do so.[4] But Harding, as with many presidents, was learning on the job. He was learning to focus his attention where it was most needed.

By early 1923 those in the cabinet with whom Harding had been closest in the early days, namely Harry Daugherty and Albert Fall, no longer had the same influence with him. Rather, the president relied principally on Hughes, Hoover, Mellon, and Wallace. It was no surprise when Albert Fall resigned his cabinet post on January 2, 1923, to be effective on March 4. Fall had told Harding of his financial problems when he had entered the cabinet.

Harding had learned he could not rely on his cabinet as a support system. Similarly, as his presidential papers show, he had learned that not every problem deserved his full attention, and increasingly he farmed out the lesser issues to the cabinet departments, or to his small staff, for resolution.

Harding may have hastened his own physical decline when he, like his entire cabinet, was hit by a particularly virulent strain of flu in early 1923. As soon as he was physically able to get out of bed, Harding returned to work. It was too soon. When Congress adjourned in March 1923, Dr. Sawyer insisted Harding go to Florida for a few days of rest. He did, but he was far from recovered when he returned to Washington after ten days in Florida. The president was having great difficulty sleeping, thus recovering. It was later written by Harding detractors that he could not sleep because of his concern about potential scandals. While this might have added to his concerns, it was not the reason he could not sleep.

The president's personal valet, Arthur Brooks, explained the president's sleeping problem to Colonel Edmund Starling, who was in charge of the Secret Service protective detail at the White House. Brooks, who was concerned, took Starling aside to tell him "something is going to happen to our boss. He can't sleep at night. He can't lie down. He has to be propped up with pillows and he sits up that way all night. If he lies down he can't get his breath."[5] Years later, medical experts concluded that Harding's flu attack had likely been accompanied by an undiagnosed heart attack. It had gone undetected because few physicians understood heart ailments at that time. Nonetheless, Harding's illness was obvious. "His normal ruddy color had become a pallor and his energies were always at low ebb."[6] Harding told Secretary Hughes his blood pressure was constantly over 175, which provoked Hughes to write his wife, "We have been worrying about Mrs. Harding, but I think it is the President we should be more concerned about."[7]

Harding's health was already failing when he got the first whiff of potential scandal. Dr. Sawyer had learned that Charles Forbes, head of the Veterans Bureau, was abusing his position. Sawyer had an interest in Forbes because his patient, Florence Harding, was deeply involved with the well-being of veterans. Sawyer had regular dealings with Forbes, who owed his job to the first lady. Her biographer, Carl Anthony, explains: "Forbes had been a frequent guest at her home and worked hard for Warren's election. She considered his credentials impeccable: He had been a commissioned Signal Corps major, earning the Croix de Guerre and the Distinguished Service Medal in the war. Besides this, he teased and flirted with her, 'making frequent passes,' which one observer rather harshly thought 'may have been a unique experience for her.'" President Harding appointed Forbes to head the War Risk

Insurance Bureau, which later became the Veterans Bureau. Will Hays and Harry Daugherty had opposed the Forbes appointment. "On having Charlie look after her boys [the wounded veterans], however, the Duchess ruled."[8]

While Florence was recuperating, Sawyer learned from the surgeon general, H. S. Cummings, that Forbes was selling warehouses filled with hospital supplies that Cummings said belonged to the Public Health Service. Sawyer informed Daugherty, who investigated and found that Forbes was indeed selling surplus supplies (sheets, towels, soap, gauze, winter pajamas, and the like), and at absurdly low prices, to private contractors in private deals. Daugherty suspected, but had no proof, that Forbes was taking kickbacks. When Daugherty informed Harding, the president summoned Forbes to the White House and demanded an explanation. Forbes lied to the president and told him the surplus materials were being sold because the annual storage cost was $650,000, which was too expensive. When Harding asked for an appraisal of the goods being sold, Forbes produced phony information. Apparently still suspicious, Harding ordered Forbes to stop his sales, and Forbes agreed in writing to do so. But Forbes continued his dubious activity. A very angry president summoned Forbes to the White House again, where Harding refused to accept his lame excuses and demanded his resignation for insubordination. Forbes pleaded innocence and begged that he be permitted to resign after he left town, claiming to have personal business in Europe. Harding granted him that, and a few days later, on February 15, 1923, the resignation arrived. By that time, word was out that Forbes had been removed because of questionable behavior, which was sufficient to get the attention of Congress.

On March 2, 1923, the U.S. Senate began investigating Forbes's activities at the Veterans Bureau. But not until after Harding's death was the extent of Forbes's criminal activity discovered. Clearly he was a crook—a foolish one to boot. Forbes had not only stolen from the government; he had stolen the young wife of one of his partners in crime. Elias H. Mortimer decided to end Forbes's affair with his wife and their European vacation by sending Forbes to jail. Mortimer provided devastating testimony about his schemes with Forbes for kickbacks on the purchases of land, and building contracts, for new veterans hospitals. Seeing the hand-writing on the wall, twelve days after the Senate inquiry had started, Charles F. Cramer, another Forbes coconspirator and the legal adviser to the Veterans Bureau, committed suicide in the bathroom of his home. In an ironic twist, Cramer had purchased the Harding home on Wyoming Avenue.

Years later, historian Robert H. Ferrell confirmed, with regard to the criminal activities at the Veterans Bureau, that Harding acted quite appropriately and that those who criticized Harding for letting Forbes slip off to Europe to resign ignored the fact that Harding did not have any evidence of Forbes's criminal activity, only his insubordination.[9] Ferrell also notes that Harding immediately appointed a new director for the Veterans Bureau, who quickly cleaned up the mess Forbes had made and proved an able administrator. One widely accepted report, which Ferrell corroborates, indicates that a reporter from the *New York Times* accidentally happened upon a portion of Harding's last encounter with Forbes. It was a memorable moment, for the six-foot-plus president had his hands on Forbes's neck and was shaking him "as a dog would a rat," while shouting, "You double-crossing bastard."[10] Harding did not live to see Forbes indicted and convicted of looting perhaps as much as $2 million from the Veterans Bureau.[11] Journalist William Allen White claimed, during an interview shortly after Forbes's departure, that Harding lamented, "I have no trouble with my enemies, I can take care of my enemies all right. But my damn friends . . . they're the ones that keep me walking the floor nights."[12]

Shortly before departing on a trip to the West Coast and Alaska, which the president had been thinking about since before the first lady became ill, the president got another whiff of trouble. The best of Harding's many sources of information were his former colleagues in the Senate. One particularly good source for Harding was GOP Senate leader James W. Wadsworth Jr. of New York, who in early 1923 passed along some ugly rumors about Harry Daugherty's close friend and private assistant Jesse W. Smith.

Smith and Daugherty were from the same uniquely named small Ohio town—Washington Court House. They had known each other since Jesse's boyhood, when the much older Daugherty became young Jesse's adviser and big brother after his father died. Daugherty had helped launch Smith into business, and Smith became a financially successful small-town department store owner in Washington Court House. There was nothing Smith would not do for Daugherty. During the 1920 campaign, Smith became Daugherty's unpaid but official gofer and was later able to entertain (and deflect) the constant stream of job seekers pursuing Daugherty after Harding's victory. Given the fact that Daugherty's wife was ill and forced to remain in Columbus, Jesse Smith set up house for Daugherty in Washington and made himself so valuable to the new attorney general that Daugherty gave him an office near his on the sixth floor of the Department of Justice, although Smith was never on the government payroll.

Jesse Smith was a bachelor, divorced from a beautiful redhead, Roxy Stimson. Rumor had it that Roxy was attracted to Jesse's money but was less than sexually satisfied by her husband, so they divorced but remained close friends. Roxy kept looking for Mr. Right, while Smith was happy as a bachelor. Jesse Smith's only connection to Harding was through Daugherty, who occasionally took him to the White House for poker games. Smith was also friendly with Florence Harding. Smith's knowledge of fabrics and women's clothing, from his years of running his successful department store, made him a favorite with women, and from time to time he assisted First Lady Florence Harding in purchasing clothing. It was rumored that Smith and Daugherty had a homosexual relationship, but there is no evidence to support the rumor.

It is not clear how much Harding learned of Smith's activities, which purportedly involved selling bonded government liquor to bootleggers. Reportedly, "Harding definitely knew about some of Jesse Smith's actions and attempted to scare him away from Washington in order to forestall his arrest and imprisonment. [But no one] will ever know how many specific details Harding had uncovered about the house on K Street, but it was enough to make him realize Smith's culpability."[13] The house at 1625 K Street, with a "greenstone facing," belonged to a newspaper editor and would-be politician from Urbana, Ohio, Howard Mannington, who had volunteered to help Harding with his 1914 Senate race. Mannington had assisted in arranging for visiting delegations to Marion during Harding's 1920 front-porch campaign. After the inauguration, Mannington ingratiated himself to Smith by helping him work his way through the mass of letters sent to Daugherty by job seekers, and soon Mannington was leading the pliable Smith astray. Smith, who had become self-important, vicariously enjoying the power and stature of his old friends, apparently became involved in petty graft with the bootleggers. There is also evidence that Smith was Daugherty's bagman. Howard Mannington, Jesse Smith, and their friends who schemed at the "little green house on K Street" later became known as the "Ohio Gang," but it was not much of a gang; rather, they were "simply a collection of rank opportunists who worked together as a matter of expediency. . . . They looked for a quick buck, and not sustained graft."[14] Harding has never been linked to any of the activities of the so-called Ohio Gang.

Clearly, Harding learned enough of Jesse Smith's activities to want him disassociated from his presidency. Daugherty had placed Smith's name on the list of persons to travel with Harding on the Alaska trip. When Harding saw Smith's name on the list, he

told Daugherty not only could Smith not make the trip, but he
wanted him out of Washington. Daugherty knew this was going to
be a heartbreaker for Smith, who had been deeply depressed following an appendectomy operation that had failed to heal properly because of his worsening diabetes. Excluding Smith from the
trip and sending him home did deepen his depression. Roxy and
Daugherty became concerned that he might take his life. It
appears that Jesse Smith tried to appeal to Harding personally on
May 29, 1923 (only days before the president's scheduled departure), but Daugherty, who was staying at the White House at the
time, blocked the effort. Precisely what happened after that is not
known. On May 29, Daugherty instructed his special assistant,
Warren F. Martin, to go to Smith's apartment and spend the night
to keep an eye on him. At 6:30 A.M. the next morning, Martin said
he heard a crashing noise and ran to check. He found Jesse Smith
dead on the floor. It appeared a suicide. Smith was wearing his
pajamas, his bloodied head had fallen tidily into a wastebasket,
and a gun was in his hand. Martin immediately notified William J.
Burns, who headed the Federal Bureau of Investigation. Burns
called the White House. Harding was immediately informed, and
he dispatched White House physician Dr. Joel Boone, who knew
Smith. A few days later Burns shipped his body back to Washington Court House for burial. Mystery has surrounded Smith's
death because there was no autopsy, and he had burned all of his
personal papers just before his death.

Many Harding biographers, based on later reports (which were
conspicuously unbalanced and negative), claim that Smith's death
had a disastrous effect on Harding, resulting in "a creeping
malaise" that affected the administration, with the death requiring
Harding and Daugherty to "pretend that nothing serious was
wrong."[15] There is no evidence, however, other than the impression of William Allen White, to suggest this ill effect on Harding,
or that the president had reason to believe anything was seriously

amiss. In fact, conflicting, if not more reliable, facts suggest exactly the opposite.

William Allen White had only a brief off-the-record visit with Harding, which he never wrote about until long after Harding's death. The personal observations of William H. Crawford, an experienced writer and journalist for the *World Work's* magazine, are at odds with those of White. Neither journalist wrote about the president's health, although White noted the president still looking haggard from his flu. Most striking, though, is that White writes about finding a totally incompetent president worried about scandals, while Crawford writes of discovering an increasingly competent president, even a "new" president, worried only about keeping the economy growing and government spending appropriately limited. In addition to White's clear bias (he acknowledges his dislike of Harding), it must be noted that he spent only a few minutes with Harding whereas Crawford visited the White House and Harding for several days.[16] Also, White's ability to reconstruct extended verbatim statements of Harding and an aide years after having such casual conversations must be questioned, for he gives no evidence of contemporaneous notes.

Crawford was first given access to Harding three months after he commenced his presidency in 1921. Crawford, a Democrat and Wilson supporter, "spent a week in the White House" taking notes and observing Harding at work. While certainly not overwhelmed by Harding, Crawford had been more favorably impressed during his first visit than he thought possible.[17] Thus, Crawford's return visit to the White House shortly before the president's Alaska trip, when he was given "the first exclusive" interview in two years for *McClure's Magazine*, was, in effect, undertaken on comparative basis.[18] And Crawford was still no Harding fan, rather a journalist "with no prejudice favorable" to Harding. His report was published in the August 1923 issue of *McClure's Magazine*, which came out in July while Harding was on his Alaska trip, and inexplicably it has been ignored by Harding's biographers (who all cite Crawford's 1921 visit). Crawford found Harding "quite a different man from the one he is popularly conceived to be. And he has discovered that his job is widely different from what *he* expected it be—different enough to make it impossible for him to carry out the rules of conducting the office which he so explicitly laid down during his campaign for the presidency." Before discussing the "new" president, Crawford recalled the old: "The picture which his political managers showed to the public was a good-natured, none-too-brilliant man, endowed with business ability, who, if elected, would limit his endeavors to managing his own job as executive officer of the government, and who was even willing to share the direction of his restricted duties with his party leaders, who were for campaign purposes called 'the best minds.' The propaganda was handled so perfectly that this picture of Harding is still the accepted likeness."

Crawford reported why the image of Harding, particularly the idea that the president was lackadaisical in his work, was mistaken. Crawford observed Harding's days firsthand. While he didn't join the president for breakfast and newspapers in the residence, he picked up Harding's day when meetings started in the Oval Office around 9:30 A.M. and usually ended around 1 P.M. In between meetings Crawford found Harding taking telephone calls or signing the constant stream of papers demanding his attention. Most days, the president entertained a guest at lunch, making it a working lunch. "On two afternoons a week, at the express command of his physicians," Crawford writes, "the President goes to the golf course* for about three hours." Harding always returned to the Oval Office after golf to deal with anything that had arisen during his absence and to sign mail. When he left the office at the day's end, he carried papers with him that needed

---

* Harding played golf as if it were an aerobic sport. He would hit his shots quickly, and walk rapidly to the next shot, and expected those playing with him to do likewise. He also conducted business when golfing.

his attention. Crawford calculated that not including golf and meals (which often were as much business as Oval Office meetings), the president was putting in "an eighty-four-hour week!" Crawford found this to be contrary to "newspapers [that] have given out the impression that the President is neglecting his official duties."

Most noticeable to Crawford was the change in Harding's governing style, which *McClure's* editors highlighted in a summary of the story: "The Warren G. Harding of 1923 is not the Warren G. Harding we knew when he was elected in 1920. A striking feature of the political trend in recent months has been the President's declaration of independence, manifest not only in his private conversations, but in his acts. In this article . . . the President is revealed as frankly confessing that his original scheme of consultation with the 'best minds' has brought him confusing counsel instead of constructive help."

In fact, Crawford observed Harding tidying up loose ends and preparing for an early campaign trip, and vacation, to the West that would mix business and pleasure. Crawford, like those planning the Alaska trip, did not realize that the president's fifteen-hour days were killing him. The president did, and when he saw his trip schedule, he called in Colonel Starling and instructed him "to go out and cut every program" they had scheduled for him, and cut them "to the bone."[19] Harding assured his Secret Service agent that he would back him up. Starling, who was accustomed to Harding's workhorse ways, later wrote, "It was the first time I had heard him express the slightest concern for his own comfort in any matter whatsoever. He had been completely the slave of his office and his friends." But Starling knew the president wasn't sleeping well, and he "looked more weary than I had ever seen him."

Florence Harding was worried too and she instructed Starling to make sure the president's doctors were nearby throughout the trip. Starling made the arrangements, as well as others that neither the president nor Mrs. Harding was told about. Dr. Sawyer was so anxious about the first lady's poor health, and whether she could survive the Alaska trip, that he arranged to have a coffin for her placed aboard the presidential train, the *Super*. In truth, more plans were made for Mrs. Harding's well-being than the president's. The president, it appears, may have sensed the worst. In anticipation of the trip, he wrote a new will and sold the *Marion Star*—after having earlier and repeatedly rejected offers.[20] It was a momentous decision, for he had always planned to return to his editor's desk after his presidency.

The trip itinerary took the *Super* to St. Louis, Kansas City, Denver, Salt Lake City, Helena, Spokane, Portland, and Tacoma; then the presidential party was to board the U.S.S. *Henderson* and continue to Alaska. Accompanying the president were Speaker of the House Frederick Gillette, Secretary of Commerce Hoover and his wife, Secretary of Agriculture Wallace and his wife, the new secretary of interior, Hubert Work, and his wife, Dr. Sawyer and his wife, George Christian and his wife, Harding's Ohio friend Malcolm Jennings and his wife, and Dr. Boone (another White House physician). Also, of course, there was support staff (secretaries and stenographers) and Secret Service agents. At each planned stop, as well as a few water stops (for the steam) along the way, the president either gave a speech or met with official delegations. His speeches dealt with subjects he had talked of during his December 1922 state of the union address, plus he further elaborated on his wish for the United States to participate in the World Court, which he had occasionally mentioned as a substitute for the League of Nations during his campaign.[21]

To those traveling with the president it was evident he was tired and not getting much rest. Rather than losing strength, however, Harding seemed to gain strength as the trip progressed. He was enjoying his bloviating, for the receptive crowds brought him to life. By the time the party reached Yellowstone National Park, Harding was in fine sprits. He was feeling too good for Florence, who gave the public a glimpse into their marriage when she publicly scolded him. The presidential party was departing from Yellowstone when a flock of attractive females stopped the president's car so they could give him flowers and a serenade. Secret Service agents tried to pry the young women from the running boards of the open car, but the president ordered that the women could sing another song. When the party started to leave, the president suggested they return later, which pushed the matter too far for the Duchess. Florence lit into her husband: "Warren, I watched you while those girls were here! It took you just as long to say good-bye to those girls as it did for you to run through three thousand tourists yesterday at Old Faithful."[22]

To fill long hours when traveling, the president played bridge or poker. One of Harding's favorite bridge partners was Secretary Hoover, and they spent long hours playing together on the trip. Hoover later wrote that Harding confided in him during the trip about the potential scandal with Jesse Smith. He asked Hoover how he would handle an incipient scandal. Hoover advised him: "Publish it, and at least get credit for integrity on your side." When Hoover inquired if Daugherty was involved, he got no answer.[23] Hoover, however, had not found this weighing heavily on the president. To the contrary, Hoover said that Harding's excitement about visiting Alaska was like that of "a school boy entering on a holiday." Harding was awed by its majestic landscapes, which he watched from the deck of the U.S.S. *Henderson* by the hour. The Alaska visit had been festive and informative. The president had wanted to see Alaska to better understand the conflicting reports he was getting from the three dozen agencies and departments that dealt with Alaskan affairs. He had enjoyed being the first president to set foot on Alaskan soil.

After visiting Alaska the president's health started to deteriorate. Reporters noticed how bad he looked when the *Henderson* arrived in Vancouver. To relax, Harding retreated to a golf course, but after only six holes he lacked the strength to continue. To hide his fatigue, he cut over to the seventeenth hole and played the eighteenth. Back at his hotel he had to lie down and rest, and that evening he ate almost nothing. He cut his speech that evening to only fifteen minutes. In Seattle the next day, he was bolstered by a warm reception at the University of Washington. It was the largest crowd of the trip. He talked about Alaska, warning that exploitation of its vast natural resources must be measured, and he presciently noted, "Alaska is destined for ultimate statehood."[24]

Those with the president urged him to cancel his remaining schedule in Seattle that evening, but he did not want to disappoint the people who had turned out to greet him. When he finally returned to the *Super* at 7:30 P.M., he was so weak he went directly to bed, complaining of upper abdominal pain and nausea. Dr. Sawyer thought it was indigestion, maybe food poisoning, but Dr. Boone, finding the president's pulse at 120 and respiration at 40, realized it was much more serious. Clearly, the president was experiencing cardiac malfunction. Harding's new interior secretary, Dr. Work, also an able physician who was in the traveling party, agreed with Dr. Boone, and Dr. Work privately wired ahead to Dr. Ray Lyman Wilbur (later president of Stanford University and head of the American Medical Association), requesting he meet the train in San Francisco with a noted heart specialist, Dr. Charles M. Cooper.[25]

Traveling to San Francisco, Harding began feeling better. The press was told he had experienced an "acute gastrointestinal attack," which is why he had canceled his schedule for Friday and the weekend in Portland, and he was going to proceed to San Francisco. The president felt well enough to dress himself when they arrived, and he refused a wheelchair. He insisted that he walk by himself to the waiting car, which took him directly to the Palace Hotel. There he became more ill, and his doctors discovered through X rays (taken earlier on the *Henderson*) and blood samples that he had bronchopneumonia. Harding refused to take his condition seriously, insisting that he take himself in and out of the bathroom and advising his doctors that he must be ready by

Tuesday to deliver a major foreign policy address he had been working on.

During the first two days at the Palace Hotel, Sawyer briefed the newsmen. It was gobbledygook because Sawyer did not know what he was doing or saying. Working behind the scenes, George Christian and Dr. Wilbur, by Monday, July 30, produced a more accurate bulletin that was released at 10:30 A.M.: "While his condition is acute, he has temporarily overstrained his cardiovascular system by carrying on his speaking engagements while ill." It was also confirmed that he had pneumonia, which at the time was deadly. To treat the ailing head of state, all the doctors knew to do was administer digitalis and caffeine during the day, sedatives at night, and pray. Dr. Wilbur privately confided to Secretary Hoover on Monday that the president's chances were "[n]ot one in ten."[26]

On Tuesday, it was obvious that there was no way Harding could deliver his foreign policy address, so Secretary Hoover released it to the newspapers. In the written speech Harding took pride in listing some fifteen major achievements of his foreign policy. But there was one more major accomplishment he wanted to add. He wanted the United States to join the World Court.[27]

Again, Harding's health showed signs of improving. The treating physicians put the best face possible on Harding's condition, with bulletins announcing that his "heart action is definitely improved" and that he "has maintained the ground he gained last night." Reporters and editors covering the president added their own hopeful spin to their stories, like the *New York Times* headline: EVERYTHING LOOKS PROMISING FOR THE PATIENT'S FULL RECOVERY FROM ILLNESS.[28] In fact, Harding was getting stronger. His lungs were clearing, and his pulse and blood pressure were improving. On Wednesday, August 1, Dr. Wilbur privately reversed his previous diagnosis, and thought the president now had a nine out of ten chance of pulling through. Harding felt so well he visited with George Christian, who was going to read another speech for him in Los Angeles, and he visited with Colonel Starling, who recorded it.

"Well, here's the colonel," the president said, after Mrs. Harding ushered Starling into the room. The president was sitting up in bed, bolstered by pillows, just as Starling had been told earlier by Brooks. "I am glad to see you back," Harding continued. "I want to thank you for the marvelous arrangements you made for me on this trip. You carried out my wishes to a T." Starling found the president weak but in good spirits. He talked about the visit to Alaska and how it had impressed him, even if he'd had bad luck at fishing and caught none. "But I'll get some down at Bill Wrigley's place," the president was sure. He instructed Starling to make arrangements for at least a ten-day stay on Wrigley's estate. "I'll leave everything to you," Harding said. Starling wished the president well and departed.[29] Harding also spoke on the telephone with his friend Malcolm Jennings, to tell him that although he was still very tired, he was "out of the woods."[30] But the president was wrong.

Warren Harding died that evening in the Palace Hotel at 7:20 P.M. It was August 2, 1923, and he was three months short of his fifty-eighth birthday. Death came while Florence Harding was reading him an article in the *Saturday Evening Post* entitled "A Calm Review of a Calm Man," by Samuel Blythe, a respected political writer who had written a thoughtful piece on the president. Blythe said that Harding was carrying five times the load of President McKinley, yet doing it calmly and in his way: "Instead of treating all molehills as mountains, as is our national manner, he expertly appraises molehills as molehills and mountains as mountains." Harding had to like what he was hearing, because it showed appreciation for how he had learned to be a more effective chief executive, and he urged Florence to continue. She did. "He doesn't struggle mightily, as have some others who have occupied his seat, with the little things, but treats them as such; and when a real emergency comes along he gets actions as quickly, quicker in many cases, than some of his much-lauded strenuous predecessors."[31]

The announced cause of death was "apoplexy stroke." It stunned the world. At the time of his death no president was more popular and admired. The *Super*, with Harding's sarcophagus surrounded by flowers and elevated to be visible from the railroad car's windows, returned the president's body to Washington, D.C. This trip, reported in every newspaper in the land, resulted in a public outpouring of sentiment the likes of which had not been experienced by the nation since the death of Abraham Lincoln, and would not occur again until the death of Franklin Roosevelt. An estimated 9 million people from factories and farms, schools and shops, in the cities and in the fields, spontaneously appeared along the railroad tracks to silently—and often in tears—pay last respects to a president they admired, a friend they'd lost. People stood at road crossings, they formed lines in fields, they peered from rooftops, they filled windows of office buildings and crowded onto porches of homes to see the train carrying the president. Rich and poor, young and old, white and black, all reverently watching, many kneeling, with veterans of the Civil War and World War I honoring their fallen commander in chief with a final salute. Unforgettable for those on the train was how the crowds along the way all sang the president's favorite hymn, with its haunting title refrain, "Nearer My God to Thee."

With his death, even Harding's editorial critics attested to his "sincerity and high-minded purpose," many calling him "a martyr to the presidency" because of his devotion to his job. "All agreed on his gentleness, his patience, and his tolerance. He was, they said, 'an ideal American,' 'the greatest commoner since Lincoln,' and 'a Man of the people.'"[32] The *San Francisco Chronicle* of August 3, 1923, was typical with its solicitous salutation:

> President and man, statesman and friend, Warren Harding is gone. . . . As truly as any soldier who laid down his life in the smoke and flames of war Warren Harding died on the battlefield. His way was not in the tumult of battle. In the difficult paths of peace, he carried the standard and the honor of the country he loved, moving unfalteringly

forward as that love guided him. . . . Great as were the tasks
a nation set for him, the tasks he set for himself were infi-
nitely greater. He looked far beyond the moment. He
dreamed of a greater America than an America of transitory
power. . . . For Warren Harding there was no North, no
South, no East, no West. For him, there was only an undi-
vided soul that was America. Warren Harding dies as he
would have wished to die, his hand still on his task, his ardor
for service still glowing. He died as he had lived, coura-
geously, cheerfully, facing death as he faced life. America has
lost a great President. She has lost a great man.

Not all journalists felt so charitable toward Harding even in
death. For example, H. L. Mencken, who had long thought
"Gamaliel," as he liked to call Harding, the perfect "booboisie"—
one of those small-town and rural Americans who Mencken considered stupid and gullible. In an unpublished appraisal written in
the wake of Harding's death, and found in the morgue of the *Baltimore Sun*, Mencken recorded his thoughts.[33] While Mencken
had nothing nice to say about any president, the vitriol he mus-
tered after Harding's death exceeded anything he had written
while Harding was alive, but he was collecting and resurrecting
themes that had been used to discredit Harding when campaigning for the presidency, and by his detractors during his presidency.
These themes have dominated the image of Harding in history:

The funeral orgies over the most amiable of Presidents
being over at last and the members of his entourage having
vanished into the folk whence they came, it becomes possible, perhaps, to consider his career realistically without
violating decorum, and even to speculate discreetly upon
the view that posterity will take of him. Certainly no man
ever passed into the Eternal Vacuum to the tune of more
astonishing rhetoric. The Associated Press dispatches,

printed . . . during the ghastly progress of the funeral train, were not merely eloquent; they were downright maudlin. They gurgled; they snuffled; they moaned. Whoever wrote them is a supreme master of bilge.

For I can see no evidence . . . that Mr. Harding was a great and consecrated man, loved this side of idolatry by the plain people and destined to go down into history in a purple halo. The plain fact is that the plain people took little interest in him until he fell ill and died, and that even then their emotions were held very well in check, and seemed to be far more polite than poignant. And the plain fact is that he leaves behind him a career so horribly bare of achievement, and also so bare of intelligible effort, that the historians will have to labor, indeed, to make him more than a name. What did he accomplish in life? He became President. What else? I can think of absolutely nothing, save the one thing that he gave English, a new barbarism. He was, from first to last, an obscure man, even as President. No salient piece of legislation bears his name. He led no great national movement. He solved no great public problem. He said nothing arresting and memorable. A kindly and charming man, honestly eager for popularity, he lacked the qualities which awaken the devotion of multitudes.[34]

Within a few months of Harding's death the now-infamous Teapot Dome scandal erupted and Harding's fall began.[35] Teapot Dome is the name of an oil field in Salt Creek, Wyoming, so named because of a teapot-shaped rock formation that stands atop a subterranean geological dome that contains oil. The catchy and unforgettable name Teapot Dome (like Watergate a half century later) became an identifying label for a scandal associated with the leasing of this Wyoming oil field, along with others in California.[36] In 1912, President Taft had made these oil fields part of the federal government's oil reserves. In 1920, before Harding had been elected and at the behest of conservationists, Congress directed that President Wilson's secretary of the navy (who was pro-conservation) administer these oil reserves for the benefit of the navy and national security. After Harding assumed office, and in response to his requests to all his cabinet for recommendations to improve the operations of government, Navy Secretary Edwin Denby, joined by Interior Secretary Albert Fall, recommended to Harding that he issue an executive order, giving the interior secretary power to administer the oil reserves, including the leasing of these fields to commercial interests.[37] On May 31, 1921, Harding issued the requested executive order. By the spring of 1922 rumors were circulating that the Teapot Dome oil reserve had been leased to commercial interests, which was one of the worst nightmares of the conservationists. By April 15, 1922, the conservationists stirred their friends in Congress, and the Senate passed a resolution calling for Navy Secretary Denby and Interior Secretary Fall to report what had been done with the oil reserves.

Denby and Fall had leased not only the Teapot Dome site but the reserves at Elk Hills and Buena Vista, California. The leases had been secretly undertaken for national security reasons, and before the president's successful disarmament conference. Before the disarmament treaties, the Department of Navy was concerned about having sufficient oil reserves for its battleships (which would soon all be burning oil rather than coal), particularly in the Pacific, because of the powerful Japanese navy. Paralleling the national security problem, there were reports that the commercial oil-drilling operations adjacent to the California reserves had caused losses of the government's oil by drainage. Simply stated, adjacent commercial oil wells were draining oil from the underground pools and depleting the government's reserves. It was also believed that drainage could occur at the Wyoming site as well.

Secretary Fall, at the request of and in consultation with Secretary Denby and the navy command, had negotiated lease arrangements with private oil companies that provided the navy with refined oil for storage (in exchange for crude), as well as agreements to build oil storage facilities for both the Pacific and Atlantic. These arrangements had been made and consummated between November 1921 and early April 1922. By the time the Senate sought information in April 1922, the disarmament agreements had been reached, and the national security issues somewhat resolved.

Leasing the oil reserves outraged conservationists. The Senate responded on April 29, 1922, by passing a resolution authorizing the Committee of Public Lands and Surveys to undertake an investigation. To quell concern, and at Fall's behest, President Harding advised the Senate in a formal message that Secretaries Denby and Fall had submitted these matters to him and that they had his "entire approval." After that not much happened. For the next eighteen months, the man heading the investigation, Senator Thomas J. Walsh, a Democrat from Montana, gathered information and studied it. Walsh held no public hearings until October 1923, after Harding's death.

When the hearings commenced there was so little interest that Senator Walsh initially had trouble mustering a quorum of his committee. After a few technical witnesses appeared, former interior secretary Fall appeared. He was a forceful witness, and it was difficult to fault his explanation of the leasing arrangements with companies headed by experienced oil men Edward Doheny and Harry Sinclair. Most observers thought the matter was resolved. But Senator Walsh kept pushing because he had been provided background information by Albert Fall's political enemies in New Mexico, who said that Fall's Three Rivers Ranch suddenly started prospering in 1922, when Fall paid off back taxes and purchased an adjoining property that enhanced his water rights. A financially strapped Fall had become flush, and Walsh wanted to know why. When Walsh found the answer his hearings exploded into front-page stories—the Teapot Dome scandal.

At a second appearance before Walsh's committee, Edward Doheny, the longtime friend of Fall's who had been granted leasing rights to the California reserves, testified that he had "loaned" Fall $100,000 in cash, which Doheny's son Edward Jr. had carried to Fall's apartment in a black satchel. Fall's granting a lease to Harry Sinclair was also suspect, because Fall was working for Sinclair as his lawyer. The leases reeked of bribery, and Walsh wanted the federal government to prosecute. But Walsh was suspect of the Department of Justice, which was still headed by Harry Daugherty, and Walsh was not sure that Daugherty would really investigate or prosecute. To get around Daugherty, Walsh decided to have the Senate pass a resolution calling for President Coolidge to appoint a special counsel to investigate and prosecute any crimes. Daugherty, who had men monitoring the committee's activities, appears to have tipped off Coolidge, who beat Walsh to the draw.[38] Coolidge issued a statement at midnight on January 27, 1924, announcing his decision to select two special prosecutors, a Republican and a Democrat. Attorney General Daugherty also moved preemptively and sent a telegram to Coolidge at 11:25 P.M. that evening, just before the president released his statement, stating he was withdrawing the Justice Department regarding the matter because he had served in the cabinet with Fall and Denby and therefore had a conflict of interest.

Actually, Coolidge was trying to move Daugherty out of his cabinet, and his decision to appoint special counsel hastened Daugherty's departure. After Coolidge made his announcement, Daugherty's critics in the Senate smelled blood and pounced. Senator Burton Wheeler, another Montana Democrat, not only wanted Daugherty to resign; he wanted the Senate to investigate whether Daugherty too was involved in the oil leases, and he wanted to know about Daugherty's involvement with Jesse Smith and Charles Forbes, as well as all the other rumors by then circulating about Daugherty. By a vote of 66 to 1, the Senate approved the investigation of Daugherty. And on March 28, 1924, when

Daugherty resisted opening his files to the Senate inquiry, Coolidge demanded his resignation.

Notwithstanding the fact that Republicans controlled the Senate, two Democrats from Montana were turned loose to investigate the Harding presidency from stem to stern. Senate Democrats, plus many Republicans, saw both institutional and political opportunity in launching investigations in three areas of the Harding administration: hospital construction by the Veterans Affairs Department under Charles Forbes, the leasing of government oil reserves, and Harry Daugherty. These investigations produced other investigations and a general frenzy of congressional investigative activity, many with accompanying sensational public hearings. The congressional activity was followed by a steady stream of headline-producing civil and criminal court proceedings, which would continue for a decade.

None of these investigations, however, implicated Warren Harding in any corrupt activity or wrongdoing. Nonetheless, Harding was blamed for much that had gone wrong, and much had, in fact, gone wrong. Clearly Charles Forbes was a crook who had looted the Veterans Bureau. Daugherty, notwithstanding years of investigation, was never convicted of anything, which does not mean he was innocent. Daugherty was indicted for receiving money relating to the deposition of alien property. Twice the government tried Daugherty; the first time there was a hung jury and the second time the jury acquitted him. Daugherty had been indicted along with Colonel Thomas W. Miller, a former congressman and war hero with impeccable credentials not unlike Charles Forbes, who Harding appointed to head the Office of Alien Property (which handled property acquired during the war). Colonel Miller, also like Forbes, succumbed to temptation by illegally transferring a German-owned American subsidiary of American Metal Company to a syndicate that paid him $50,000 and Jesse Smith $224,000, of which $50,000 ended up in a joint account belonging to both Smith and Daugherty. Colonel Miller was convicted and sentenced to eighteen months in prison. While Daugherty was never convicted, needless to say, his already troubled reputation was ruined when he refused to explain his joint account with Smith, and what had become of the money.

As the congressional hearings and criminal proceedings were taking place, the Teapot Dome special prosecutors pursued Albert Fall, Edward Doheny, and Harry Sinclair criminally and civilly. First they succeeded in canceling the leases of the government oil reserves to Doheny's and Sinclair's companies. Then the prosecutor proceeded criminally. Albert Fall was indicted and tried for conspiring with Doheny and Sinclair but was acquitted. Then in separate criminal trials, Doheny and Sinclair were found *not* guilty of bribing Fall. However, Sinclair was imprisoned, for contempt of the Senate (refusing to answer questions) and contempt of court (hiring a detective to follow jurors). Because Albert Fall had been too ill to stand trial with Doheny, he was later tried for bribery (notwithstanding the fact that both Doheny and Sinclair had been found not guilty of bribing him). Fall was convicted in 1931 and became the first former cabinet officer to go to prison, where he served some nine months. The Teapot Dome special prosecutors needed almost a decade to complete this work.

The fact that Harding had done nothing wrong and had not been involved in any criminal activities became irrelevant. The endless stream of negative headlines about two of his cabinet officers and his purported Ohio friends took its toll. It created a climate and a market for critical—and unfortunately often unfounded—appraisals and accounts of the Harding administration, which soon made Harding little more than a punch line. Harding's reputation became inseparable from the bad apples in his administration. Their disgrace became his disgrace. All that he had done well was attributed to others, from his wife to the able men with whom he had surrounded himself. It was not the headlines or news accounts that hurt Harding. Rather, the cultural tastemakers

and political writers who later played up these stories set the stage for Harding's descent into history's dustbin.

First there were fictional accounts that were widely believed to be based on fact, such as F. Scott Fitzgerald's play *The Vegetable* (1923) and the roman à clef by Samuel Hopkins Adams entitled *Revelry* (1926). Both of these respected writers present a Harding-like president as a hapless leader too weak to deal with his corrupt cronies. Separating fact from fiction became impossible. For example, when reviewing *Revelry* the popular *Book Review Digest* observed: "It is a narrative of what went on in Washington during the Harding administration."[39] And Heywood Broun, writing in the *Nation*, claimed that *Revelry*, like Harriet Beecher Stowe's *Uncle Tom's Cabin*, which had spread the "truth" of slavery, was actually better than fact because "a novel fires the imagination far more than a news report."[40]

Early nonfiction works about Harding, many close to fiction, were even more damning. These works confirmed that the lackluster and hapless president of fiction was in fact incompetent, lazy, and lecherous. Journalists and authors who claimed inside information believed they could write with utter abandon about Harding because less than six months after the president's death, in early 1924, reports surfaced that Mrs. Harding (with the assistance of the president's military aide) had burned all of her husband's papers. The Library of Congress had sought the papers for their collections, and Frank N. Doubleday wanted to publish select portions of them. Mrs. Harding told these men she had burned the papers to protect her husband's memory. Her actions, however, accomplished the exact opposite. Believing no records existed, writers felt free to write the Harding history as they wished, and they did.

The trashing of Harding's personal life began with an alleged bang, so to speak, when Nan Britton published her purported confessional, *The President's Daughter,* in 1927. With Teapot Dome and other Harding-connected scandals still in the headlines, Britton's sense of timing to cash in could not have been better. This pretty woman, who was thirty-one years younger than Warren Harding, wrote that she became infatuated with Harding at fourteen years of age. Then, after he was elected to the U.S. Senate, and when she was twenty-three, they began a relationship that resulted in the birth of Elizabeth Ann, their daughter. According to Britton the relationship continued until Harding's death, with trysts at the White House being arranged by a trusted Secret Service agent who once pounded on a closet door in the Oval Office to warn them that Florence Harding was approaching. Britton wrote that Harding had never seen his daughter, and the refusal of his brothers and sisters to help support the child had forced her to write her tell-all. Reputable publishing houses refused to publish the book, but with the help of unidentified backers, she self-published. At first the book languished, with reviewers avoiding it and bookstores refusing to stock it. Then H. L. Mencken legitimized the book with a favorable review, and it took off, selling more than 100,000 copies and becoming the talk of the nation.

The fundamental question about the Britton book is its veracity. Ms. Britton certainly does not make the case in her book, nor was she ever able to offer anything to establish Harding's paternity of Elizabeth Ann. Many people who knew Nan in Marion believe that she got most of her information from the estranged daughter of Carrie Phillips (who did have an affair with Harding) and then created her own story. There is much evidence that Britton's claims are not possible. In his myth-busting effort to right the record about Harding, Professor Ferrell collected all the available evidence that *The President's Daughter* is more fiction than fact. He shows the gaping holes in her story, none greater than the fact that Harding lamented to his close friends and family that he was sterile and sadly could not have children, for he loved them. While she was alive, many historians corresponded with Nan Britton, with the hope of resolving the reliability of her contentions. They were unable to find viable support for her claims, however.

I reviewed Nan Britton's papers, which she bequeathed to the University of California at Los Angeles and were opened in 2000. There is nothing in her personal papers that corroborates her claims. All that her papers show is her lifetime fixation with Harding and her unending effort to have him as the father of her child.* Based on correspondence she had with various historians, it is also apparent that her papers are not complete. It is clear that Harding had an extramarital affair with Carrie Phillips, which ended while he was in the Senate, but there is no evidence that Harding had any extramarital affairs while president. Nor is there any confirmable evidence that Harding had any other affairs during his marriage.[41]

Following Britton's book a trio of popular and influential journalists, all Harding critics, commenced a new round of attacks on the Harding presidency: William Allen White in *Masks in a Pageant* (1928), Frederick Lewis Allen in *Only Yesterday: An Informal History of the Nineteen-Twenties* (1931), and Samuel Hopkins

---

* Given the fact that it is now possible to use DNA to inexpensively and conclusively establish paternity, and posthumously through siblings and their families, it occurred to me that there is an easy way to resolve this question. Professor Ferrell reports that in 1964, when the Harding papers were opened by the Ohio Historical Society, Nan Britton's daughter, Elizabeth Ann, identified herself to a *Los Angeles Times* reporter. She said she had married Henry E. Blaesing in September, 1938, and after living in the Midwest had moved to California. In 1964 she was living in Glendale, the mother of three boys. Thus, it would appear, given the offspring of Harding's siblings, and Elizabeth Ann's children, there is ample DNA to resolve Warren Harding's paternity. While the Harding family remains prominent in Ohio (a remarkable number of them following in Phoebe and Tyron Harding's footsteps by becoming physicians), I was unable to locate Elizabeth Ann or her children before completing this book. I have added this note with the hope that if I don't find them, maybe they will find me—or someone else interested in resolving this historical question.

Adams (who had earlier written the fictional work *Revelry*) in *The Incredible Era: The Life and Times of Warren G. Harding* (1939). Employing conjecture, surmise, or worse (often blatant falsehoods), they each produced remarkably unbalanced and unfair accounts, exaggerating the negative, assigning responsibility to Harding for all wrongs, and denying him credit for anything done right. Today there is considerable evidence refuting their portrayals of Harding.[42] Yet the myth has persisted.

Along with these less than fair and accurate accounts, there were several so-called insider accounts complementing Nan Britton's work, with none more sensational and astounding than that of Gaston Means's book *The Strange Death of President Harding* (1930). This was an "as told to" written by May Dixon Thacker and based on the alleged diaries of Gaston Means, who was billed as an "Ex–Department of Justice Investigator" and "star witness for the United States Government" in the sensational investigations of Teapot Dome and later of former attorney general Harry Daugherty. The book oozes with sleaze, corruption, and graft that Means claims he was involved with for the president and first lady, and it ends with an astounding claim that Mrs. Harding had poisoned her husband in San Francisco in revenge for his adultery. Even though the book's author, Ms. Thacker, later repudiated the book and confirmed that Means was every bit the notorious liar and con man others had claimed, many of his baseless contentions survive to this day.

Alice Roosevelt Longworth wrote that "Harding was not a bad man. He was just a slob."[43] She never explains why one of the best-dressed, always immaculately groomed presidents was a "slob." Nor is it likely she could, for others refute Harding being either crude or slovenly, as they do her descriptions of his White House as having "the atmosphere [of the] back room in a speakeasy."[44] It is true that Harding served liquor in the residence of the White House during Prohibition, for he, like most affluent Americans, had accumulated a good stock of it before the Eighteenth Amendment had gone into force. White House chief usher Ike Hoover describes the president's White House poker sessions as including the who's who of Washington, and when they played, they began "immediately after dinner . . . until twelve-thirty or one o'clock."[45] Colonel Starling reports that Harding never took more than one drink, a highball. "The stakes were modest, since these men played purely for the sport of it. How could Andy Mellon, for instance, get a kick out of winning money in a poker game? They played with great zest and good humor, drank moderately and sociably, and smoked—all in the best tradition of the Elks Club." Starling said he had "attended all of these gatherings" and had never seen "the slightest sign of debauch. So far as the President was concerned he could not have drunk more if he wanted to. He suffered from stomach trouble, and was allergic to alcohol in any but small doses."[46] But such facts have never hampered Harding mythmakers.

Throughout the years of partisan attacks by the Senate, then the court proceedings where prosecutors further muddied the picture to obtain convictions, followed by book after book trashing Harding, the former president found himself without defenders. His former aides and cabinet officers, men like President Calvin Coolidge, Chief Justice William Taft, and Secretary of Commerce and later President Herbert Hoover, all who knew better, remained mute, apparently afraid to speak out lest they be tarnished because of their association with Harding. Gaston Means's book did, however, stir Harding's controversial attorney general Harry Daugherty to publish his book *The Inside Story of the Harding Tragedy* (1932). Daugherty claimed he wanted to set the record straight about Samuel Adams's *Revelry*, Nan Britton's *The President's Daughter*, and Gaston Means's *The Strange Death of President Harding*. However, the less-than-credible Daugherty devotes most of his book to making himself the genius responsible for Warren Harding's political successes by embellishing and distorting his true role. Obviously, Daugherty was unaware that the

Harding papers would one day surface to impeach his claims and correct the record.

Harding's history was mostly written sans historians. Historians, who want primary source material (particularly documentary records), long believed none existed for the Harding presidency. Accordingly, historians for many years ignored the Harding era. But by the mid-1930s (a decade after the deaths of both President and Mrs. Harding) rumors started circulating that maybe Mrs. Harding had not, in fact, destroyed all her husband's papers. And by the early 1940s it was widely known that indeed Harding's papers did exist, although they were still not available and no one was sure how extensive they might be. Harding researcher Ray Baker Harris, writing for the Ohio Historical Society in 1943, told historians that it had "been erroneously stated, and is still repeated by writers occasionally, that Mrs. Harding destroyed all of her husband's papers. This is completely untrue."[47] Harris reported that, in fact, a significant collection of Harding's papers was in the possession of the Harding Memorial Association, which (with limited resources) was slowly inventorying and cataloging the material. "It is safe to say," Harris added, "that whenever the Harding papers are made available, many of those who have written so glibly and even sensationally of President Harding's later life [referring to his Senate and White House years] will be happy that their work has long since been forgotten."[48] On this assessment, Harris was wrong. Those glib and sensational works have not been forgotten; rather they remain at the core of the received history of the Harding years. But he was correct about the existence of the papers.

Notwithstanding Mrs. Harding's instructions to George Christian, the president's private secretary, to pack up all the president's papers and ship them to her in Marion, Christian did not follow her orders. Rather, he sent her only a few boxes of material in addition to what she had taken herself from the president's office. Christian said nothing and stored the bulk of the material in the basement of the White House, where it was not discovered until 1929 (during the Hoover administration). Florence Harding, who died a little over a year after her husband, never knew that Christian had left behind one hundred cubic feet of records from Harding's presidency. In addition, he had kept all the records of Harding's six years in the U.S. Senate and the 1920 presidential campaign, which he had stored in his own home in Marion. By 1935, all these papers were in the basement of Harding's Marion home, where they remained for three more decades unprocessed and unavailable due to lack of interest and lack of funds. In addition, Harding's friends at the Harding Memorial Association remained concerned about what might be in the papers, so they were reluctant to do anything with them. For Harding, and history, it proved a terrible mistake.

When historians tried to obtain access to the Harding papers, the Harding Memorial Association, under the control of Dr. Carl Sawyer, the son of Warren and Florence Harding's White House (and longtime) physician, refused all requests. But as the hundredth anniversary of Warren Harding's birth approached in the early 1960s, the Harding Memorial Association (impressed with the professionalism of the Ohio Historical Society) finally agreed to transfer the papers to the Ohio Historical Society in Columbus. In late October 1963 the papers were moved to the Ohio Historical Society's building by a moving van accompanied by armed Ohio State Patrol cars. It seems Dr. Carl Sawyer feared a possible hijacking by "those Teapot Dome people."[49] Working with remarkable dispatch the Ohio Historical Society cataloged and prepared the papers for public use, opening them on April 25, 1964.

The collection is substantial, with 907 document boxes filling 226 feet of shelf space and containing approximately 350,000 items. By 1970 this material had been microfilmed and today can be found in some fifteen university libraries throughout the United States. While there are a few gaps, these documents provide solid evidence about the character, thinking, and activities of Warren Harding and his brief administration. This material presents a strikingly different picture of the Harding presidency than his detractors had painted. For example, when Randolph Downes, then editor of the *Northwest Ohio Quarterly*, began research on his Harding biography, he was "so shocked at the contemptuous and degrading things unfairly said about Harding" that he wrote a lengthy article (in 1967) laying out and highlighting almost four decades of distortions about Harding. His title makes the point: "The Harding Muckfest: Warren G. Harding—Chief Victim of the Muck-for-Muck's Sake Writers and Readers." Downes concluded his essay with a plea: "It is saddening to relate this perversion, this poisoning of the wells of American history. There is much that we must unlearn lest we become hypnotized with false learning that is worse than ignorance. . . . It is high time for a painstakingly honest and scholarly appraisal of the life of Warren G. Harding."[50] Unfortunately, there has been little unlearning about Warren Harding and there are very few published studies based on the Harding Papers that can be called painstakingly honest and scholarly appraisals. Dr. Ferrell concluded his Harding study with the observation that "[h]istory . . . is sometimes thoughtless about the people who make it." And he believes that Harding has been ranked at the bottom of ranking polls by historians because his colleagues have simply ignored the evidence.[51]

With Harding's death in 1923, there was renewed talk of Secretary of State Charles Evans Hughes becoming president, for he had distinguished himself at the State Department. But Hughes would next distinguish himself at the U.S. Supreme Court by returning to become chief justice from 1930 to 1941. As the ranking member of Harding's cabinet, it fell to Hughes to deliver the memorial eulogy. Hughes's friends urged him "to tone down his estimate of his dead chief" in the address he had drafted but "[h]e refused to change a word, for in writing the speech he had drawn

only upon his personal knowledge of Harding."[52] His memorial address to the joint session of Congress on February 28, 1924, was characteristically eloquent. Mrs. Harding later wrote to Hughes that she could not have wished him to change a single sentence, and Chief Justice Taft thought it the best memorial of the many he had heard during his long career.[53]

Hughes talked of the solid and substantial accomplishments of Harding's unfinished presidency, and of Harding's policies that would become the basis of the Coolidge presidency.[54] Hughes spoke of the man he had come to know and admire, who was "completely and typically American. He was neither helped nor hampered by exceptional environment. He suffered neither from poverty nor from riches. His endowment was a keen mind and a strong body. Alert to opportunity, self-reliant, facile, and warmhearted, he made his own way, owing his successes to his tireless persistence and his unquenchable ardor in living." The secretary of state, albeit tactfully, even addressed Harding's weakness when explaining "[h]e literally wore himself out in the endeavor to be friendly. It was pain to him to refuse a courtesy; personal convenience could never be considered if it was an obstacle to any act of grace. He dealt personally with a vast correspondence, not being content with the mere acknowledgements, but writing friendly letters with the touch of keen human interest. His generous receptivity multiplied the appeals. He sought relaxation in the intimate contacts of old friendships, and this led him even in his diversions often to give himself to an undue exertion instead of rest."

Hughes reported that when Harding had been stricken in San Francisco, and was told that "the gravity of his condition" could mean he might not be able to resume "the routine of his labors," Harding had exclaimed: "Well, if that is so, this story might as well come to an end." And it did, Hughes said, "in a moment of apparent refreshment, there was a slight movement and he was gone." Hughes closed with these appropriate lines:

Let who has felt compute the strain
Of struggle with abuses strong,
The doubtful course, the helpless pain
Of seeing best intents go wrong.
We, who look on with critic eyes,
Exempt from action's crucial test,
Human ourselves, at least are wise
In honoring one who did his best.[55]

Notes

INTRODUCTION

1. Andrew Sinclair, *The Available Man: Warren Gamaliel Harding* (New York: The Macmillian Company, 1965), 297.
2. Robert K. Murray, *The Harding Era: Warren G. Harding and His Administration* (Minneapolis: University of Minnesota Press, 1969), 536–37.
3. When working on this book I learned that Florence Harding was the great-grandmother of my childhood friends Peter and David De Wolfe.

1: YOUNG HARDING

1. Carl Sferrazza Anthony, *Florence Harding: The First Lady, The Jazz Age, and the Death of America's Most Scandalous President* (New York: William Morrow, 1998), 35.
2. Ibid.
3. Francis Russell, *The Shadow of Blooming Grove: Warren G. Harding in His Times* (New York: McGraw Hill Book Company, 1968), 43.
4. Ibid., 39.
5. George L. Edmunds, "My Boy Warren: The Father's Story of the President-Elect and His Success System," *McClure's Magazine* (March 21, 1921), 23.

6. Randolph C. Downes, *The Rise of Warren Gamaliel Harding: 1865–1920* (Columbus: Ohio State University Press, 1970), 7.

7. Ibid., 9–10.

8. Russell, *The Shadow of Blooming Grove*, 46.

9. Willis Fletcher Johnson, *The Life of Warren G. Harding: From the Simple Life of the Farm to the Glamour and Power of the White House* (Philadelphia: The John C. Winston Company, 1923), 20.

10. John J. McCusker, "Comparing the Purchasing Power of Money in the United States (or Colonies) from 1665 to Any Other Year Including the Present," Economic History Services, 2001, URL: http://www.eh.net/hmit/ppowerusd/

11. Ray Baker Harris, "Background and Youth of the Seventh Ohio President," *Ohio History*, vol. 52, July/September 1943, 274.

12. Ibid.

13. http://www.infidels.org/library/historical/robert_ingersoll/

14. Russell, *The Shadow of Blooming Grove*, 57.

2: EDITOR, PUBLISHER, AND APPRENTICE POLITICIAN

1. Carl Sferrazza Anthony, *Florence Harding: The First Lady, The Jazz Age, and the Death of America's Most Scandalous President* (New York: William Morrow, 1998), 3–108.

2. Ibid., 9.

3. Ibid., 27.

4. Ibid., 41.

5. Historians have treated this subject not unlike most relating to Harding, with few seeking the truth and many distorting it. For example, Francis Russell makes Harding's rumored black ancestry the backdrop, subtext, and implicit title of his 1968 Harding biography, *The Shadow of Blooming Grove*, and he claims it explains Harding's psychological makeup. In a rare footnote in the book, Russell halfheartedly refutes the truth of the gossip (which he has labeled "the shadow" of Blooming Grove) as improbable if not impossible.

6. Randolph C. Downes, *The Rise of Warren Gamaliel Harding: 1865–1920* (Columbia: Ohio State University Press, 1970), 554–55.

7. Robert K. Murray, *The Harding Era: Warren G. Harding and His Administration* (Minneapolis: University of Minnesota Press, 1969), 64.

8. Downes, *The Rise of Warren Gamaliel Harding*, 28.

9. Anthony, *Florence Harding*, 58.

10. Joe Mitchell Chapple, *Life and Times of Warren G. Harding* (Boston: Chapple Publishing Co., Ltd., 1924), 53–54.

11. See Anthony, *Florence Harding*, 48–49.

12. Andrew Sinclair, *The Available Man: Warren Gamaliel Harding* (New York: The Macmillian Company, 1965), 286.

13. Chapple, *Life and Times of Warren G. Harding*, 69–70.

14. An appropriate term used repeatedly in the writings of Randolph C. Downes.

15. Ellis Grey Boatman, "Evolution of a President: The Political Apprenticeship of Warren G. Harding" (Ph.D. diss., University of South Carolina, 1966), 27.

16. See the Harding Papers, microfilm edition assembled by Archives and Manuscripts Division, Ohio Historical Society (1970), Marion Papers (1888–1920), Senatorial Papers (1915–1921).

17. George MacAdams, "Harding," *World's Work* 40 (October 1920): 618.

18. See Downes, *The Rise of Warren Gamaliel Harding*, 96–133; and Sinclair, *The Available Man*, 33–46.

19. Anthony, *Florence Harding*, 79–80.

20. Ibid., 79.

21. Ibid., 84.

22. Boatman, "Evolution of a President," 43.

23. Ibid.

24. Ibid., 45.

25. Ibid.

26. Ibid., 46.

27. Downes, *The Rise of Warren Gamaliel Harding*, 177.

28. Ibid., 176.

29. Alice Roosevelt Longworth, *Crowded Hours: Reminiscences of Alice Roosevelt Longworth* (New York: Charles Scribner's Sons, 1933), 202–3.

3: UNITED STATES SENATOR

1. Randolph C. Downes, *The Rise of Warren Gamaliel Harding: 1865–1920* (Columbus: Ohio State University Press, 1970), 192.

2. Ellis Grey Boatman, "Evolution of a President: The Political Apprenticeship of Warren G. Harding" (Ph.D. diss., University of South Carolina, 1966), 40–41.

3. Carl Sferrazza Anthony, *Florence Harding* (New York: William Morrow, 1998), 108.

4. Joe Mitchell Chapple, *Life and Times of Warren G. Harding* (Boston: Chapple Publishing Co.), 90.

5. Boatman, "Evolution of a President," 54.

6. Downes, *The Rise of Warren Gamaliel Harding*, 201.

7. Boatman, "Evolution of a President," 54.

8. Ibid.

9. Ibid., 56.

10. Downes, *The Rise of Warren Gamaliel Harding*, 215.

11. W. Dale Nelson, *Who Speaks for the President? The White House Press Secretary from Cleveland to Clinton* (Syracuse: Syracuse University Press, 1998), 40.

12. Merlo J. Pusey, *Charles Evans Hughes*, vol. 1 (New York: The Macmillan Company, 1951), 322.

13. Arthur M. Schlesinger Jr., Fred L. Israel, and William P. Hansen (eds.), *History of American Presidential Elections 1789–2001*, vol. VI (1912–1924), "Election of 1916," Appendix (Philadelphia: Chelsea House Publishers, 2002), 2345.

14. Eugene P. Trani and David L. Wilson, *The Presidency of Warren G. Harding* (Lawrence: University Press of Kansas, 1977), 35.

15. Andrew Sinclair, *The Available Man* (New York: The Macmillan Company, 1965), 222.

16. Harding Papers, Rolls 26–27.

17. Henry Cabot Lodge, *The Senate and the League of Nations* (New York: Charles Scribner's Sons, 1925), Appendix IV.

18. See Lodge, *The Senate and the League of Nations*, Appendix IV, for a stenographic record of the August 19, 1919, White House conference.

19. *Congressional Record,* Senate, September 11, 1919, vol. LVIII, part 5, 5219–25.

20. Ibid., 5225.

21. Boatman, "Evolution of a President," 130.

22. Anthony, *Florence Harding,* 167.

4: WINNING THE NOMINATION

1. Randolph C. Downes, *The Rise of Warren Gamaliel Harding: 1865–1920* (Columbus: Ohio State University Press, 1970), 354.

2. Harding Papers (letter to L. C. Breunig, May 18, 1920).

3. Ellis Grey Boatman, "Evolution of a President" (Ph.D. diss., University of South Carolina, 1966), 79.

4. Warren G. Harding, *Our Common Country* (Indianapolis: Bobbs-Merrill Co., 1921), 64–65.

5. Boatman, "Evolution of a President," 136.

6. Harding had 123,257 votes to Wood's 108,565 but he failed to control the entire delegation. Of the forty-eight delegates to the convention, Harding won thirty-nine delegates while Wood had captured nine.

7. The final tally gave General Wood 85,708 votes, Hiram Johnson received 79,840 votes, Frank Lowden had 39,627 vote, with Harding garnering only 30,782 votes.

8. Samuel Hopkins Adams, *Incredible Era: The Life and Times of Warren Gamaliel Harding* (Boston: Houghton Mifflin Company, 1939), 125–26.

9. Downes, *The Rise of Warren Gamaliel Harding,* 411.

10. Ibid., 406–10.

11. Boatman, "Evolution of a President," 194.

12. Ibid.

13. Arthur M. Schlesinger Jr., Fred L. Israel, and William P. Hansen (eds.), *History of American Presidential Elections 1789–2001,* vol. VI (1912–1924), "Election of 1920," Appendix (Philadelphia: Chelsea House Publishers, 2002), 2405.

14. Carl Sferrazza Anthony, *Florence Harding* (New York: William Morrow, 1998), 185.

15. Ibid., 171–88.

16. Downes, *The Rise of Warren Gamaliel Harding*, 388 (citing the *New York Times*, February 21, 1920).

17. Ray Baker Harris, "Warren G. Harding: An Account of His Nomination for the Presidency by the Republican Convention of 1920" (Washington, D.C.: privately published, 1957), 15.

18. Boatman, "Evolution of a President," 249.

19. Ibid., 248.

20. Ibid., 264.

21. Ibid., 265.

22. Wesley M. Bagby, *The Road to Normalcy: The Presidential Campaign and Election of 1920* (Baltimore: Johns Hopkins Press, 1962), 194.

23. Harry M. Daugherty with Thomas Dixon, *Inside Story of the Harding Tragedy* (Boston: Western Islands, 1975; reprint of 1932 edition), 49.

24. Reported in Nicholas Murray Butler, *Across the Busy Years* (New York: Charles Scribner's Sons, 1935), vol. 1, 279.

25. Boatman, "Evolution of a President," 278.

26. See Bagby, *The Road to Normalcy*, 213–18.

5: THE 1920 CAMPAIGN

1. August Heckscher, *Woodrow Wilson* (New York: Charles Scribner's Sons, 1991), 633.

2. Arthur M. Schlesinger Jr., Fred L. Israel, and William P. Hansen (eds.), *History of American Presidential Elections 1789–2001*, vol. VI (1912–1924) (Philadelphia: Chelsea House Publishers, 2002), 2364–65.

3. Wesley M. Bagby, *The Road to Normalcy: The Presidential Campaign and Election of 1920* (Baltimore: Johns Hopkins Press, 1962), 463.

4. John A. Morello, *Selling the President, 1920: Albert D. Lasker, Advertising, and the Election of Warren G. Harding* (Westport, Conn.: Praeger, 2001), 4, 15, 27–28.

5. Joe Mitchell Chapple, *Life and Times of Warren G. Harding: Our After-War President* (Boston: Chapple Publishing Company, 1924), 120

6. Bagby, *The Road to Normalcy*, 482.

7. Wayne R. Whitaker, "Warren G. Harding and the Press" (Ph.D. diss., Graduate College of Ohio University, 1972), 65.

8. Robert K. Murray, *The Harding Era: Warren G. Harding and His Administration* (Minneapolis: University of Minnesota Press, 1969), 52.

9. Bagby, *The Road to Normalcy*, 465.

10. William G. McAdoo, *Crowded Years* (Boston: Houghton Mifflin Company, 1931), 389.

11. Paul F. Boller Jr., *Presidential Anecdotes* (New York: Oxford University Press, 1981), 229.

12. Whitaker, "Warren G. Harding and the Press," 68–73.

13. Ibid., 41.

14. Andrew Sinclair, *The Available Man: Warren Gamaliel Harding* (New York: The Macmillan Company, 1965), 161.

15. Randolph C. Downes, *The Rise of Warren Gamaliel Harding 1865–1920* (Columbus: Ohio State University Press, 1970), 557.

16. Sinclair, *The Available Man*, 170.

17. Downes, *The Rise of Warren Gamaliel Harding*, 554.

18. Whitaker, "Warren G. Harding and the Press," 92–96.

19. Sinclair, *The Available Man*, 167.

20. Bagby, *The Road to Normalcy*, 601 (citing the *New York Times* of July 10, 15, September 15, October 19, 30, and November 2, 1920).

21. Schlesinger et al., *History of American Presidential Elections*, 2456.

22. Murray, *The Harding Era*, 91.

23. Bagby, *The Road to Normalcy*, 606.

24. Sinclair, *The Available Man*, 176–77.

25. Whitaker, "Warren G. Harding and the Press," 107–8.

6: CABINET MAKING

1. Randolph C. Downes, *The Rise of Warren Gamaliel Harding, 1865–1920* (Columbus: Ohio State University Press, 1970), 586.

2. Edmund W. Starling (as told to Thomas Sugrue), *Starling of the White House: The Story of the Man Whose Secret Service Detail*

Guarded Five Presidents from Woodrow Wilson to Franklin D. Roo-sevelt (New York: Simon and Schuster, 1946), 169.

3. Alice Roosevelt Longworth, *Crowded Hours: Reminiscences of Alice Roosevelt Longworth* (New York: Charles Scribner's Sons, 1933), 322.

4. Carl Sferrazza Anthony, *Florence Harding: The First Lady, The Jazz Age, and the Death of America's Most Scandalous President* (New York: William Morrow, 1998), 241. In examining president-elect Harding's cabinet selections, I have drawn on the overviews found in Andrew Sinclair, *The Available Man: Warren Gamaliel Harding* (New York: The Macmillian Company, 1965), 183–89; Eugene P. Trani and David L. Wilson, *The Presidency of Warren G. Harding* (Lawrence: University Press of Kansas), 38–48; Joe Mitchell Chapple, *The Life and Times of Warren G. Harding: Our After-War President* (Boston: Chapple Publishing Co.), 131–39; and the sources more specifically cited below.

5. Nan Kathryn Jamieson Lowerre, "Warren G. Harding and American Foreign Affairs, 1915–1923" (Ph.D. diss., Stanford University, 1968), 75.

6. Ibid., 78.

7. Richard B. Morris, *Encyclopedia of American History* (New York: Harper & Brothers, 1953), 331.

8. Trani and Wilson, *The Presidency of Warren G. Harding*, 39.

9. See Sinclair, *The Available Man*, 183–87; Trani and Wilson, *The Presidency of Warren G. Harding:* 38–47; and Chapple, *Life and Times of Warren G. Harding*, 131–39.

10. Sinclair, *The Available Man*, 185.

11. Robert K. Murray, *The Harding Era: Warren G. Harding and His Administration* (Minneapolis: University of Minnesota Press, 1969), 101.

12. Ibid.

13. Trani and Wilson, *The Presidency of Warren G. Harding*, 13.

14. See Murray, *The Harding Era*, 103–4; Trani and Wilson, *The Presidency of Warren G. Harding*, 3, 41; and the Department of Labor (www.dol.gov/asp/programs/history/davis.htm).

15. Trani and Wilson, *The Presidency of Warren G. Harding*, 43–44.

16. David H. Stratton, *Tempest Over Teapot Dome: The Story of Albert B. Fall* (Norman: University of Oklahoma Press, 1998), 197.

17. Samuel Hopkins Adams, *The Incredible Era: The Life and Times of Warren Gamaliel Harding* (Boston: Houghton Mifflin Company, 1939), 202.

18. Stratton, *Tempest Over Teapot Dome*, 202.

19. E.g., Nelson W. Polsby, "Presidential Cabinet Marking: Lesson for the Political System," *Political Science Quarterly* 93 (spring 1978).

20. Robert K. Murray, "President Harding and His Cabinet," *Ohio History: The Scholarly Journal of the Ohio Historical Society* 75 (spring/summer 1966): 124.

7: AN UNFINISHED PRESIDENCY

1. Robert K. Murray, *The Harding Era: Warren G. Harding and His Administration* (Minneapolis: University of Minnesota Press, 1969), 92.

2. Ibid.

3. *Political Science Quarterly* 38 Supp. (September 1923): 26, 35.

4. Lindsay Rogers, "American Government and Politics: The First (Special) Session of the Sixty-Seventh Congress April 11, 1921–November 23, 1921," *The American Political Science Review* 16 (February 1922): 41–52.

5. Eugene P. Trani and David L. Wilson, *The Presidency of Warren G. Harding* (Lawrence: University Press of Kansas, 1977), 55.

6. Joe Mitchell Chapple, *Life and Times of Warren G. Harding: Our After-War President* (Boston: Chapple Publishing Company, 1924), 170; Wayne R. Whitaker, "Warren G. Harding and the Press" (Ph.D. diss., Graduate College of Ohio University, 1972), 131, 138.

7. Whitaker, "Warren G. Harding and the Press," 132.

8. Ibid., 174; Murray, *The Harding Era*, 273–74.

9. Murray, *The Harding Era*, 114.

10. Ibid., 126.

11. *Congressional Record*, 67th Congress, 1st session, vol. LXI, part 1, 172.

12. John De Novo, "The Culbertson Economic Mission and Anglo-American Tension in the Middle East, 1944–1945," *The Journal of American History* 63 (March 1977): 913, n16.

13. Murray, *The Harding Era*, 273–74.

14. Harding Papers, Roll 240.

15. See, e.g., Barry Eichengreen, "The Origins and Nature of the Great Slump Revisited," *The Economic History Review* 45:2 (May 1992).

16. Trani and Wilson, *The Presidency of Warren G. Harding*, 63.

17. Ibid., 70–73.

18. Charles Kettleborough, "Soldiers' Bonus," *The American Political Science Review* 16 (August 1922): 455.

19. Trani and Wilson, *The Presidency of Warren G. Harding*, 64–65; *Congressional Record*, 67th Congress, 1st session, vol. LXI, part 4, 3597–98.

20. *Congressional Record*, 67th Congress, 1st session, vol. LXI, part 4, 3600.

21. Murray, *The Harding Era*, 187.

22. Trani and Wilson, *The Presidency of Warren G. Harding*, 78–79.

23. Edward L. Schapsmeier and Frederick H. Schapsmeier, "Disharmony in the Harding Cabinet: Hoover-Wallace Conflict," *Ohio History* 75 (spring/summer 1966): 128–29.

24. Trani and Wilson, *The Presidency of Warren G. Harding*, 90.

25. Harding Papers, Roll 240.

26. Schapsmeier and Schapsmeier, "Disharmony in the Harding Cabinet," 131.

27. Ibid.

28. See, e.g., David P. Claiborne, "The Perils of the Capper-Volstead Act and Its Judicial Treatment: Agricultural Cooperation and Integrated Farming Operations," *Willamette Law Review* (spring 2002): 287.

29. Schapsmeier and Schapsmeier, "Disharmony in the Harding Cabinet," 131–32.

30. Lindsay Rogers, "American Government and Politics: The Second, Third, and Fourth Session of the Sixty-Seventh Congress," *The American Political Science Review* 18 (February 1924): 92.

31. Rogers, ". . . Second, Third, and Fourth Session of the Sixty-Seventh Congress," 91.

32. Murray, *The Harding Era*, 128.

33. Randolph C. Downes, *The Rise of Warren Gamaliel Harding 1865–1920* (Columbus: Ohio State University Press, 1970), 78.

34. W. H. Crawford, "Introducing Our New President," *McClure's Magazine* (August 1923): 33.

35. Murray, *The Harding Era*, 238.

36. Harding Papers, Roll 240.

37. Murray, *The Harding Era*, 233.

38. "Sinister Issues Involved in the Coal Strike," *Current Opinion* 72 (May 1922): 577.

39. Murray, *The Harding Era*, 246; Trani and Wilson, *The Presidency of Warren G. Harding*, 96–101.

40. Edmund Morris, *Theodore Rex* (New York: Random House, 2001), 168–69.

41. Harding Papers, Roll 240.

42. Ibid.

43. Murray, *The Harding Era*, 248.

44. See Colin J. Davis, *Power at Odds: The 1922 National Railroad Shopmen's Strike* (Urbana: University of Illinois Press, 1997).

45. Harding Papers, Roll 241.

46. Murray, *The Harding Era*, 252.

47. See generally Davis, *Power at Odds*.

48. Ibid., 130.

49. Ibid., 134.

50. See Henry J. Abraham, *Justices, Presidents and Senators: A History of the U.S. Supreme Court Appointments from Washington to Clinton* (New York: Rowman & Littlefield Publishing, Inc., 1999), 139–45.

51. Richard B. Sherman, "The Harding Administration and the Negro: An Opportunity Lost," *Journal of Negro History* 49 (July 1964): 156.

52. Ibid., 168.

53. Robert Ellwood Hauser, "Warren G. Harding and His Attempts to Reorganize the Republican Party in the South, 1920–23" (Ph.D. diss., Pennsylvania State University, 1973), 258–60.

54. Ibid., 260.

55. Sherman, "The Harding Administration and the Negro," 167.

56. Hauser, "Warren G. Harding," 261–62.

57. Harding Papers, Roll 240; Murray, *The Harding Era*, 399–401.

58. August Heckscher, *Woodrow Wilson* (New York: Charles Scribner's Sons, 1991), 643.

59. Harry Daugherly, with Thomas Dixon, *The Inside Story of the Harding Tragedy* (Boston: Western Islands, 1975; reprint of 1932 edition), 110.

60. See Murray, *The Harding Era*, 167 and 169.

61. Andrew Sinclair, *The Available Man: Warren Gamaliel Harding* (New York: The Macmillan Company, 1965), 226.

62. Francis Russell, *The Shadow of Blooming Grove: Warren G. Harding in His Times* (New York: McGraw Hill Book Company, 1968), 463.

63. Daugherty, *The Inside Story of the Harding Tragedy*, 108.

64. Murray, *The Harding Era*, 169.

65. Nan Kathryn Jamieson Lowerre, "Warren G. Harding and American Foreign Affairs, 1915–1923" (Ph.D. diss., Stanford University, 1968), 92–93.

66. Elizabeth Jaffray, *Secrets of the White House* (New York: Cosmopolitan Book Corporation, 1927), 81.

67. *Congressional Record*, 67th Congress, 1st session, vol. LXI, part 8, 7665–66.

68. Ibid., 7666.

69. Lowerre, "Warren G. Harding and American Foreign Affairs," 96.

70. Ibid., 121–22 (citing historians Harold and Margaret Sprout and State Department legal adviser Chandler P. Anderson).

71. See Fred I. Greenstein, *The Hidden-Hand Presidency: Eisenhower as Leader* (Baltimore: Johns Hopkins University Press, 1982 and 1994), and Fred I. Greenstein, "Ronald Reagan. Another Hidden-Hand Ike?" *PS: Political Science and Politics* 23:1 (March 1990): 7–13.

72. H. H. Kohlsaat, *From McKinley to Harding: Personal Recollections of Our Presidents* (New York: Charles Scribner's Sons, 1923), 231–32.

73. See Carl Sferrazza Anthony, *Florence Harding* (New York: William Morrow, 1998), 378–88.

8: DEATH AND DISGRACE

1. Harding Papers, Roll 240.

2. Robert K. Murray, *The Harding Era: Warren G. Harding and His Administration* (Minneapolis: University of Minnesota Press, 1969), 378, 575.

3. Ibid., 417.

4. Ibid., 418.

5. Edmund M. Starling (as told to Thomas Sugrue), *Starling of the White House: The Story of the Man Whose Secret Service Detail Guarded Five Presidents from Woodrow Wilson to Franklin D. Roosevelt* (New York: Simon and Schuster, 1946), 189.

6. Murray, *The Harding Era*, 439.

7. Ibid.

8. Carl Sferrazza Anthony, *Florence Harding* (New York: William Morrow, 1998), 244–45.

9. Robert H. Ferrell, *The Strange Deaths of President Harding* (Columbia: University of Missouri Press, 1996), 121.

10. Ibid.

11. Andrew Sinclair, *The Available Man: Warren Gamaliel Harding* (New York: The Macmillan Company, 1965), 261.

12. Francis Russell, *The Shadow of Blooming Grove: Warren G. Harding in His Times* (New York: McGraw Hill Book Company, 1968), 560.

13. Murray, *The Harding Era*, 484.

14. Ibid., 434.

15. Ibid., 437. (Murray also appears to rely principally on William Allen White and Nicholas Murray Butler, both of whom had less than objective views of Harding.)

16. For William Allen White's bias, see Walter Johnson (ed.), *Selected Letters of William Allen White* (New York: Henry Holt and Company, 1947), 260.

17. W. H. Crawford, "A Democratic View of Our Three-Months' President," *Current Opinion* 6. (June 1921): 757.

18. W. H. Crawford, "Introducing Our New President: Mr. Harding Now Declares His Independence of the 'Best Minds,'" *McClure's Magazine* (August 1923): 30.

19. Starling, *Starling of the White House*, 195.

20. Murray, *The Harding Era*, 440–41.

21. See Joe Mitchell Chapple, *Life and Times of Warren G. Harding: Our After-War President* (Boston: Chapple Publishing Company, 1924), 326–75.

22. Anthony, *Florence Harding*, 428.

23. Murray, *The Harding Era*, 447.

24. Ibid., 448.

25. Ibid, 447–51. The account of Harding's final days and hours is also based on material found in Robert H. Ferrell, *The Strange Deaths of President Harding* (Columbia, University of Missouri Press, 1996), 31–49; and Sinclair, *The Available Man*, 284–87.

26. Ferrell, *The Strange Deaths of President Harding*, 17.

27. Murray, *The Harding Era*, 449.

28. Ferrell, *The Strange Deaths of President Harding*, 17.

29. Starling, *Starling of the White House*, 198.

30. Murray, *The Harding Era*, 449.

31. Samuel G. Blythe, "A Calm Review of a Calm Man," *Saturday Evening Post*, July 28, 1923. Harding Papers, Roll 259.

32. Murray, *The Harding Era*, 457.

33. Journalist and novelist Roy Hoopes located the Mencken essay when undertaking research for his novel *Our Man in Washington* (New York: Tom Dorherty Associates, 2000). It is also quoted (without attribution or explanation) in Randolph C. Downes, "The Harding Muckfest: Warren G. Harding—Chief Victim of the Muck-for-Muck's Sake Writers and Readers," *Northwest Ohio Quarterly* 39 (summer 1967): 5–37.

34. See H. L. Mencken (edited by Malcolm Moos), *A Carnival of Buncombe: Writings on Politics* (Chicago: The University of Chicago Press, 1884), 1–60.

35. See Louis W. Potts, "Who Was Warren G. Harding?" *The Historian* 34 (August 1974): 621–45.

36. See Burt Noggle, *Teapot Dome: Oil and Politics in the 1920s* (Westport: Greenwood Press, Publishers, 1980); David H. Stratton, *Tempest Over Teapot Dome: The Story of Albert B. Fall* (Norman: University of Oklahoma Press, 1998); Margaret Leslie

Davis, *Dark Side of Fortune: Triumph and Scandal in the Life of Oil Tycoon Edward L. Doheny* (Berkeley: University of California Press, 1998); and M. R. Werner and John Starr, *Teapot Dome* (New York: The Viking Press, 1959). See also, *Mammoth Oil Company et al. v. United States,* 275 U.S. 13 (1927); *Sinclair et al. v. United States,* 279 U.S. 749 (1929); and *Fall v. United States,* 49 F.2d 506 (1931).

37. *Fall v. United States,* 49 F.2d 506 (1931).

38. See Leslie E. Bennett, "One Lesson from History: Appointment of Special Counsel and the Investigation of the Teapot Dome Scandal," Brookings Institute Study (http://www.brook.edu/).

39. Downes, "The Harding Muckfest," 10.

40. Ibid., 11.

41. Nor is there anything but the weakest hearsay to support the contentions of some historians that Harding had other affairs as well as other children.

42. See, e.g., Randolph C. Downes, *The Rise of Warren Gamaliel Harding: 1865–1920* (Columbus: Ohio State University Press, 1970), 446–47.

43. Alice Roosevelt Longworth, *Crowded Hours: Reminiscences of Alice Roosevelt Longworth* (New York: Charles Scribner's Sons, 1933), 325.

44. Ibid.

45. Irwin Meed Hoover, *Forty-two Years in the White House* (Boston: Houghton Mifflin Company, 1934), 250.

46. Starling, *Starling of the White House,* 169–70.

47. Ray Baker Harris, "Background and Youth of the Seventh Ohio President," *Ohio History: The Scholarly Journal of the Ohio Historical Society* 52 (July/September 1943): 275.

48. Ibid.

49. Francis Russell, "A Naughty President," *The New York Review of Books,* June 24, 1982.

50. Downes, "The Harding Muckfest," 34.

51. Ferrell, *The Strange Deaths,* 165–67.

52. Merlo J. Pusey, *Charles Evans Hughes,* vol. 2 (New York: The Macmillan Company, 1951), 566–67.

53. Ibid.
54. Robert K. Murray, *The Politics of Normalcy: Government Theory and Practice in the Harding-Coolidge Era* (New York: W. W. Norton & Co., 1973), 130–46.
55. Chapple, *Life and Times of Warren G. Harding*, Appendix, 309–25.

Milestones

1865 Born near Blooming Grove, Ohio

1882 Graduated from Ohio Central College

1884 Purchased *Marion Star* newspaper

1891 Married Florence Kling De Wolfe

1900–4 Member of Ohio State Senate

1904–5 Lieutenant governor of Ohio

1910 Unsuccessful bid for governor of Ohio

1912 Nominating speech for President Taft at GOP convention

1914 Elected to the United States Senate

1917 United States enters World War I

1919 Death of former president Theodore Roosevelt
President Wilson submits Treaty of Versailles and League of Nations to the U.S. Senate
President Wilson suffers an incapacitating stroke (September)

1920 Elected president of the United States

1921 Signed Budget and Accounting Act of 1921 and Immigration Per Centum Act of 1921
Created Department of Veterans Affairs
Washington Conference on Unemployment
Appointed Taft as chief justice of Supreme Court
Pardoned Eugene V. Debs

1921–22 Washington Disarmament Conference

1922   Washington Conference on Agriculture
        Nationwide coal miners' strike; Coal Commission created
        Nationwide railroad strike; Attorney General Daugherty
        obtained injunction from federal judge James Wilkerson to
        end rail strike
1923   Died in San Francisco
        Scandal investigations of the Veteran Affairs Bureau and
        Teapot Dome (Wyoming) oil lease begin

Selected Bibliography

UNPUBLISHED MATERIALS

Boatman, Ellis Grey. "Evolution of a President: The Political Apprenticeship of Warren G. Harding." Ph.D. diss., University of South Carolina, 1966.

Harding, Warren G. Warren G. Harding Papers. Ohio Historical Society in Columbus, Ohio (microfilm, California State University, Hayward, Library).

Hauser, Robert Ellwood. "Warren G. Harding and His Attempts to Reorganize the Republican Party in the South, 1920–23." Ph.D. diss., Pennsylvania State University, 1973.

Lowerre, Nan Kathryn Jamieson. "Warren G. Harding and American Foreign Affairs, 1915–1923." Ph.D. diss., Stanford University, 1968.

Whitaker, Wayne R. "Warren G. Harding and the Press." Ph.D. diss., Ohio University, 1972.

BOOKS

Adams, Samuel Hopkins. *The Incredible Era: The Life and Times of Warren Gamaliel Harding.* Boston: Houghton Mifflin Company, 1939.

Anthony, Carl Sferrazza. *Florence Harding: The First Lady, The Jazz*

Age, and the Death of America's Most Scandalous President. New York: William Morrow, 1998.

Bagby, Wesley M. *The Road to Normalcy: The Presidential Campaign and Election of 1920.* Baltimore: Johns Hopkins Press, 1962.

Britton, Nan. *The President's Daughter.* New York: Elizabeth Ann Guild, Inc., 1927.

Chapple, Joe Mitchell. *Harding the Man.* Boston: Chapple Publishing Co., 1920.

————. *The Life and Times of Warren G. Harding: Our After-War President.* Boston: Chapple Publishing Co., 1924.

Cottrill, Dale. *The Conciliator.* Philadelphia: Dorrance, 1969.

Daugherty, Harry M., with Thomas Dixon. *The Inside Story of the Harding Tragedy.* Boston: Western Islands, 1975 (reprint of 1932 edition).

Davis, Colin J. *Power at Odds: The 1922 National Railroad Shopmen's Strike.* Urbana: University of Illinois Press, 1997.

Downes, Randolph C. *The Life of Warren Gamaliel Harding, 1865–1920.* Columbus: Ohio State University Press, 1970.

Ferrell, Robert H. *The Strange Deaths of President Harding.* Columbia: University of Missouri Press, 1996.

Harris, Ray Baker. "Warren G. Harding: An Account of His Nomination for the Presidency by the Republican Convention of 1920." Washington, D.C., privately published, 1957.

Noggle, Burt. *Teapot Dome: Oil and Politics in the 1920's.* Westport: Greenwood Press, Publishers, 1980.

Murray, Robert K. *The Harding Era: Warren G. Harding and His Administration.* Minneapolis: University of Minnesota Press, 1969.

————. *The Politics of Normalcy: Government Theory and Practice in the Harding-Coolidge Era.* New York: W. W. Norton & Co., 1973.

Russell, Francis. *The Shadow of Blooming Grove: Warren G. Harding in His Times.* New York: McGraw Hill Book Company, 1968.

Sinclair, Andrew. *The Available Man: Warren Gamaliel Harding.* New York: The Macmillian Company, 1965.

Sullivan, Mark. *Our Times: The United States, 1900–1925,* 6 vols. New York: Charles Scribner's Sons, 1926–1935.

Trani, Eugene P., and David L. Wilson. *The Presidency of Warren G. Harding.* Lawrence: University Press of Kansas, 1977.

ARTICLES

Crawford, W. H. "A Democratic View of Our Three-Months' President." *Current Opinion* (June 1921): 757–60.

——— "Introducing Our New President." *McClure's Magazine* (August 1923): 30–35.

Downes, Randolph C. "The Harding Muckfest: Warren G. Harding— Chief Victim of the Muck-for-Muck's Sake Writers and Readers." *Northwest Ohio History* 39 (1967): 5–37.

Schapsmeier, Edward L., and Frederick H. Schapsmeier. "Disharmony in the Harding Cabinet: Hoover-Wallace Conflict." *Ohio History* 75 (spring/summer 1966): 126–36, 188–90.

Sherman, Richard B. "The Harding Administration and the Negro: An Opportunity Lost." *Journal of Negro History* 49, no. 3 (July 1964): 151–68.

Wright, Quincy. "The Washington Conference." *The American Political Science Review* (May 1922): 285–97.

Index

Adams, Samuel Hopkins
  *The Incredible Era: The Life and
    Times of Warren G. Harding,*
    163–64
  Revelry, 161
African heritage rumors, 19–20,
    74–76
agricultural conference, January
    23, 1922, 112
Alaska trip, health decline during,
    147–50
alien property scandal,
    159–60
Allen, Frederick Lewis, 163
Americanism speeches, 55
Anthony, Carl (on Florence
    Harding)
  De Wolfe affair, 15–18
  friendship with Charles Forbes,
    139
  health, 25–26
  near death experience, 135
  predictions of Madame Marcia,
    61
Arthur, Chester, 11

biographer, of Florence Harding.
    See Anthony, Carl (on
    Florence Harding)
biographers, of Warren G. Harding
  Downes, Randolph, 35, 114, 168
  Murray, Robert, 1, 19–20, 95, 99
  Randolph Downes, 114
  Sinclair, Andrew, 87
  Trani, Eugene, 44–45
  Wilson, David, 44–45
Birmingham speech (1921),
    125–26
Blackstone Hotel conference,
    GOP convention (1920),
    63–64
Blaesing, Elizabeth Ann, 162, 163
Blaine, James, 11–12
Britton, Nan
  The President's Daughter, 3,
    161–63
  unfounded allegations, 161–63
Bryan, William Jennings, 21
Budget and Accounting Act, 1921,
    105
"Bull Moose" Party, 30–31

Bureau of the Budget, 85, 105–6
Burton, Theodore E., 33
Butler, Nicholas Murray, 53
Butler, Pierce, 122

cabinet appointments, 82–94
  advisors, 82
  Agriculture, 84
  Commerce, 86
  confirmations, 92–94
  Interior, 90
  Justice, 90–92
  Labor, 88–89
  Navy, 89, 92
  Post Office, 89
  State, 82–84
  Treasury, 84–87
  War, 87
cabinet, new precedents in role of,
  97–98
campaign (1910), Ohio governor
  defeat, 28
  Republican Party split, 27–28
  Taft's support, 28
  Theodore Roosevelt's support,
  27
campaign, presidential
  finances scandal, 58–59
  issues, 74–76
  manager, 51–52
  strategy, 51–52
campaign, U.S. Senate race, 35
Chancellor, William E., 75–76
Charles Forbes scandal. See Forbes,
  Charles (scandal)
Christian, George
  Harding Papers, 166–67
  as personal secretary, 37–38
  as presidential aide, 38

civil rights legislation
  antilynching legislation,
  123–24
  Birmingham speech (1921),
  125–26
coal miners' strike (1922)
  John L. Lewis's role in, 116
  labor demands, 115
  negotiations, 116–17
Colby, Bainbridge, 68
Cole, Ralph, 35
Congress, 67th special session
  Congressional address, April 12,
  1921, 100–101
  emergency tariffs, 97, 102–4
  farm related legislation, 111–13
  immigration law, 101–2
  tax reform, 97, 106–10
Coolidge, Calvin
  as presidential aspirant, 53
  as presiding officer, Senate,
  92–93
  role in Harding's presidential
  campaign, 71
  role in scandal investigation,
  158
  vice presidential nomination, 67
Cox, James M., 68, 69
Cramer, Charles F., 141
Crawford, William H., 145–47

Daugherty, Harry M.
  anti-union position, 117
  as attorney general, 90–91
  canvassing delegates' votes, 65
  deadlock strategy at GOP
  convention, 57–58
  as Harding's campaign manager,
  51–52

The Inside Story of the Harding Tragedy, 165–66
political fixer, 50–51
presidential campaign, 69
role in alien property scandal, 159
role in GOP convention (1920), 59, 61–62
role in Harding's U.S. Senate race, 33–35
Davis, James J., 88–89
Davis, Colin J., 120–21
Dawes, Charles G.
  Bureau of the Budget, 85, 105–6
  credentials, 84–85
De Wolfe, Pete, 2, 16–18
Debs, Eugene
  clemency granted to, 126–29
  presidential election, 1912, 30
  presidential election, 1920, 77
Democratic convention, 1920, 68–69
Democratic presidential campaign, 1920, 71–72
Denby, Edwin N., 92, 93, 156–57
Doheny, Edward, 157–58, 160
Donithen, Hoke, 35
Downes, Randolph
  appraisal of Harding, 168
  Harding's campaign style, 35
  Harding's labor views, 114
Du Bois, W. E. B., 126

Fall, Albert B.
  bribery conviction, 160
  as secretary of the interior, 90, 93
  Teapot Dome scandal, 156–58, 160
  as U.S. Senator, 39

Ferrell, Robert H., 141, 168
Fletcher, Henry P., 83–84
Foraker, Joseph, 35
Forbes, Charles (scandal)
  denial of charges, 140
  Robert Ferrell on, 141
  Senate investigation, 140–41, 159
  Veterans Bureau and, 139
foreign policy, 129–35
  of Charles E. Hughes, 129–30
  return to "normalcy," 129
  Washington disarmament conference, 131–35
front-porch campaign, 69, 72

Garford, Arthur L., 36
Garvey, Marcus, 126
Gompers, Samuel, 88
GOP convention (1884)
  "mugwumps," 12
  Chester Arthur and, 11
  contenders, 11–12
  Harding, as *Marion Star* editor, 10–12
GOP convention (1912)
  Republican Party split, 28–29
  support of Taft, 30–31
GOP convention (1920). *See* nomination campaign (1920)

Harding Papers
  burned, 161
  found, 167–68
  preserved, 166–67
  Ray Baker Harris as researcher, 166

Harding, Florence, 15–23
　affair with Pete De Wolfe, 2,
　　16–18
　biographer of. *See* Anthony, Carl
　　(on Florence Harding)
　childhood, 15
　conflict with father, 16–20
　courtship, 18–20
　death of father, 34
　health of, 25–26
　marriage, 20–23
　near death experience, 135–36
　reconciliation with father, 27
　relationship with Carrie
　　Wallace, 16–17
　schooling, 15–16
　Senate acceptance, 80
　support at GOP convention,
　　1920, 60–61
　support during nomination
　　campaign, 51
　visit with Lady Edith Wilson,
　　81–82
Harding, Warren G.
　affair with Carrie Phillips, 35
　African heritage rumors, 19–20,
　　74–76
　biographers of. *See* biographers,
　　of Warren G. Harding
　Carrie Phillips affair, 26–27
　death, 152–55
　early jobs, 9–12
　early political career. *See*
　　political career, early
　education, 7–9
　friendship with George
　　Christian, 37–38
　health, 22
　marriage, 20–23

mistress, 2
newspaper career. *See*
　newspaper career (Harding's)
nomination campaign (1920).
　See nomination campaign
　(1920)
parents of, 5–6
party loyalty, 34
personality, 24
presidential campaign. *See*
　presidential campaign
relationship with Amos Kling,
　14–20
speeches. *See* speeches
Harding, Warren G., legacy. *See*
　also Harding Papers
　Alice Longworth Roosevelt on,
　　164–65
　author's comments on, 1–4
　fictional accounts of, 161
　Harry M. Daugherty on,
　　165–66
　Hughes's memorial eulogy,
　　168–70
　journalist accounts, 163–64
　lack of defense of, 165–67
　The President's Daughter and,
　　161–63
　Robert H. Ferrell on, 168
　sensational accounts, 164
　Teapot Dome scandal and,
　　155–60
Harris, Ray Baker, 166
Harvey, George, 63–64
Hays, Will
　as campaign chairman, 69
　as postmaster general, 89
　as potential presidential
　　nominee, 65

role on Republican National
Committee, 59, 63
Hogan, Timothy, 36
Hoover, Herbert
Alaska trip, 149
Palace Hotel, San Francisco, 151
as presidential aspirant, 53
as secretary of commerce, 85–86
Hughes, Charles Evans
foreign policy, 129–30
memorial eulogy by, 168–70
as Republican presidential
nominee, 39–40, 42–43
role in Washington disarmament
conference, 132–35
as secretary of state, 82–83

inaugural address, 95–96
Indiana primary defeat (Harding),
56
Ingersoll, Robert, 11–12

Jennings, Malcolm, 124, 129, 152
Johnson, James Weldon, NAACP,
123–24
Johnson, Hiram, 53, 59

Kenyon, W. S., 58–59
Kling, Amos (father-in-law)
conflict with Florence, 16–20
death, 34
reconciliation with Florence, 27
relationship with Warren G.
Harding, 14
Kling, Florence Mabel. See
Harding, Florence

labor unrest, 114–21
address to Congress, 117–19

coal miners' strike, 1922,
115–16
pro-labor legislation, 115
railroad shop workers strike,
116–19
Wikerson federal injunction,
119–20
Lasker, Albert D., 69–70
Laylin, Lewis C., 32
League of Nations
as campaign issue, 71–72
Woodrow Wilson's role in,
47–50
legacy, Harding's. See Harding,
Warren G., legacy
Lewis, John L., 116
Lodge, Henry Cabot
as convention chairman, 1920,
59, 63
opposition to League of
Nations, 47–48, 49
as Republican leader in Senate,
80
role in cabinet selection, 82,
86–87
Lowden, Frank O.
cabinet proposal, 89, 92
campaign finance scandal,
58–59
Lowerre, Nan Jamieson, 129–30,
133

marriage
Amos Kling's opposition, 18–20
courtship, 20–23
Maxwell, Jack, 3
McAdoo, William Gibbs, 68
McKinley, William, campaign of, 23
Means, Gaston, 164, 165

Mellon, Andrew, 86–87
Mencken, H. L.
    on Harding's death, 154–55
    on Harding's speeches, 73
    review of *The President's Daughter*, 162
Miller, Thomas W., 159–60
Moton, Robert R., 126
Murray, Robert
    on African heritage rumors, 19–20
    on Harding Papers, 1
    on Harding's relationship with press, 99
    on problems facing Harding, 95

NAACP, civil rights legislation, 123–24
newspaper career (Harding's)
    Caledonia Argus, 6
    GOP convention, 1884, 10–12
    Marion Star, 10, 13–14
    return from politics, 31–32
    during term as U.S. senator, 36–37
nomination campaign (1920)
    balloting deadlock, 61–64
    Blackstone Hotel suite, 65
    breaking the deadlock, 64–66
    campaign finance scandal, 58–59
    campaign strategy, 51–52
    comments on Harding's nomination potential, 43–46
    Florence Harding's role, 51, 56–57, 60–61
    Frank Scobey's support, 46

Harding's ability to run for Senate and, 51
Harding's role on Senate Foreign Relations Committee and, 47
Harry M. Daugherty's role, 50–52, 59, 61–62
impact of Theodore Roosevelt's death, 46
League of Nations as issue, 48–49
Republican aspirants, 50, 53–54
Republican platform, 59–60
role of Ohio delegation, 62–63

Ohio Historical Society, 167–68

Palace Hotel, San Francisco, 151, 152
Per Centum Act, May 19, 1921, 101–2
Phillips, Carrie, affair with, 2, 26–27, 35
Poindexter, Miles, 54
political career, early, 23–32
    conflicts, 28–30
    disillusionment following campaign for governor, 32
    Ohio lieutenant governor, 25
    Ohio state senator, 23
    re-election, Ohio Senate, 25
    role in personality, 24
    withdrawal from political life due to wife's illness, 25
presidency, of Harding
    Alaska trip, 147–49
    Budget and Accounting Act, 1921, 105–6
    Bureau of the Budget, 105–6

Charles Forbes scandal, 139–41
civil rights legislation, 123–26
Congress, 67th special session, 97
Congress, relationship with,
    113–14
Congressional address, April 12,
    1921, 100–101
death in office, 152–55
domestic improvements, 137
Eugene Debs and, 126–29
first cabinet meeting, 97–98
Florence Harding's illness,
    135–36
foreign policy. See foreign policy
health decline, 137–38, 149–52
inaugural address, 95–96
Jesse W. Smith scandal, 142–45,
    149
labor unrest. See labor unrest
observers of, 144–47
Per Centum Act, May 19, 1921,
    101–2
president-elect, period as, 79–82
press conferences, 98–100
tariff protection, 102–5
tax cut issues, 106–10
Teapot Dome scandal, 155–60
U.S. Supreme Court
    appointments, 121–23
presidential campaign
acceptance speech, 70–71
Albert D. Lasker's role, 69–70
Calvin Coolidge as running
    mate, 71
campaign issues, 74–76
front-porch campaign, 69, 72
graciousness, 74–75
Harry M. Daugherty's role, 69
Judson C.Welliver's role, 73

press, 73–74
public relations, 69–70, 72
speeches, 70–73
Will Hays's role, 69
William E.Chancellor's
    allegations, 75–76
presidential preference primaries,
    54, 56
The President's Daughter
alleged affair, Nan Britton, 3,
    161–63
H. L. Mencken's review, 162
lack of corroboration, 163
Robert H. Ferrell comments of,
    162
Procter, William C., 55, 58
Progressive Party, 42
public relations, presidential
    campaign, 69–70, 72

railroad shop workers strike,
    116–17
Reily, E. Mont, 46–47
Republican convention, 1920. See
    nomination campaign
    (1920)
Republican Party, split in
"Bull Moose" Party, 30–31
GOP convention, 1912, 28–29
Harding's campaign for
    governor, 27–28
political conflicts, 28–30
reputation, historical. See Harding,
    Warren G., legacy
Roosevelt, Alice Longworth
criticism of Harding, 29–30,
    164–65
reconciliation, brief, 81
Roosevelt, Franklin D., 68–69

Roosevelt, Theodore
   death, 46
   GOP convention, 1884, 11–12
   political conflicts, 28–30
   return to Republican Party, 42
   support, Ohio governor race, 27
Root, Elihu, 59–60, 82
Russell, Francis, 26–27

scandals, alien property, 159–60
scandals, Charles Forbes. See
      Forbes, Charles (scandal)
scandals, Jesse W. Smith. See
      Smith, Jesse W. (scandal)
scandals, Teapot Dome. See Teapot
      Dome scandal
Scobey, Frank
   correspondence with, 45
   role in nomination campaign, 46
   Texas trip, 79
Seibold, Louis, 91–92
Senate Foreign Relations
      Committee, 47–48
Senate investigation
   of Charles Forbes, 159
   of Harry M. Daugherty, 159
   of Teapot Dome scandal,
      157–58
senator, (Harding as), 38–52
   Albert B. Fall and, 39
   Andrew Sinclair on, 45
   campaign, 33–36
   Charles Evans Hughes and,
      39–43
   first term, 44–45
   Foreign Relations Committee,
      44
   Frank Scobey's correspondence
      with Harding, 45

as junior senator, 38
   newspaper career of Harding
      and, 36–37
   nomination campaign and,
      43–46
   social life, 39
   speeches, 39–41
   tariffs, 41
Sickle, Jack, 13
Sinclair, Andrew, 45
   on Andrew Mellon, 87
   on Harding Papers, 1
   on Harding's campaign victory,
      77
   on Harding's image, 45
Sinclair, Harry, 157–58, 160
Smith, Jesse W. (scandal), 142–45
   "Ohio Gang," 143
   effect on Harding, 144–45
   friendship with Daugherty and,
      142–43
   Harding as president and,
      142–45, 149
   suicide of, 144
Smoot, Reed, 64–65
speeches
   Americanism, 55
   eulogy of McKinley, 24–25
   GOP convention, 1916, 39–41
   healing and normalcy, 57
   at Hughes's nomination, 42
   against League of Nations,
      48–49
   nomination acceptance, 70–71
   as Ohio lieutenant governor, 25
   during presidential campaign,
      72–73
   supporting McKinley's
      campaign, 23

supporting Taft's presidential
  nomination, 30–31
U.S. Senate race, 35
Sproul, William C., 53–54
Stoddard, Henry, 41
Sutherland, George, 122

Taft, William Howard
  appointment as chief justice,
    122–23
  role in Harding's nomination
    campaign, 24–25
  support for Harding in Ohio
    governor race, 28
tariff protection, 102–5
  emergency tariff statute, May
    27, 1921, 102
  Fordney-McCumber Act, Sept.
    21, 1922, 104–5
  in second state of the union
    address, 105
  Thomas Marvin's role in, 103
  William S. Culbertson's role in,
    104
tax cut issues, 106–10
  Andrew Mellon on, 106–8
  Boies Penrose on, 110
  veterans' bonus bill and, 107–9
Teapot Dome scandal, 155–60
  "Watergate," 1
  Denby, Edwin N., 156–57
  Doheny, Edward, 157–58, 160
  Fall, Albert B., 156–58, 160
  leasing oil fields, 155–57
  Senate investigation, 157–58
  Sinclair, Harry, 157–58, 160
  Walsh, Thomas J., 157–58,
    159
  Wheeler, Burton, 158–59

Thompson, Charles Willis, 36
Trani, Eugene, 44–45

U.S. Supreme Court
  appointments, 122–23

veterans' bonus bill
  clash with Senate, 107–9
  Harding's veto, 110–11
  Mellon's opposition, 108
Veterans Bureau. See Charles
    Forbes scandal

Wallace, Carrie, 16–17
Wallace, Henry C., 84, 112
Walsh, Thomas J., 157–58, 159
Warwick, Jack, 13
Washington disarmament
  conference. See foreign policy
"Watergate," 1
Weeks, John, 87
Welliver, Judson C., 73
Wheeler, Burton, 158–59
White, William Allen
  attack on Harding presidency,
    163
  on Charles Forbes scandal, 141
  personal observations of
    Harding, 144–45
Wilkerson federal injunction,
    120–21
Wilkerson, James H., 120–21
Willis, Frank B., 36
Wilson, David, 44–45
Wilson, Edith, 81–82
Wilson, Woodrow
  Democratic convention, 1920,
    68
  neutrality policy of, 40

Wilson, Woodrow (*cont'd*)
   presidential election, 1912, 30
   role in League of Nations,
     47–50
   stroke, 50
   war declaration, 45

Wood, General Leonard
   campaign finance scandal and,
     58–59
   presidential aspirations, 54
   Procter as campaign manager
     for, 55

ABOUT THE AUTHOR

———

John W. Dean served as Richard Nixon's White House counsel for a thousand days. He received a graduate fellowship from American University to study government and the presidency before entering Georgetown Law Center, where he received his JD in 1965. He is the author of two books recounting his days in the Nixon administration, *Blind Ambition* and *Lost Honor,* as well as *The Rehnquist Choice* and *Unmasking Deep Throat.* A native of Marion, Ohio, he lives in Beverly Hills, California.